I have known Israel and Brook Wayne and their children for many years. During that time I have had the joy of watching their family grow to now nine children. When it comes to parenting, they practice what they preach. Speaking from the perspective of a pastor, their children are some of the most well-behaved children I've ever had the blessing of being with. They behave better, and pay attention in church, more than some adults I know. Biblically parenting their children isn't something they just do, it's who they are. I only wish I had their insights to parenting when I raised my own. It would have made things easier.

**Richard Grom, Calvary Chapel Sunset Coast**

The Wayne's have done a wonderful job of telling a story of the danger of anger in the family. Their transparency shows they have lived in our shoes and this lends credibility to their anger solutions. If we fall to temptation and sin in the area of anger, there is hope in repentance and confession as seen in their story. I was greatly encouraged by regularly pointing us to biblical truth. One of the keys of adopting what the Waynes are teaching is that it will help to build the foundation for long-term healthy relationships with our children as they move into adulthood. I would highly recommend this book and the study questions at the end of each chapter to help overcome all forms of anger in the home.

**Todd Kangas, Director of Midwest Parent Educators**

Israel and Brook Wayne have hit one out of the ballpark with this book! *Pitchin' a Fit* is the most practical, thoughtful, and insightful book on parenting that I have read. There is so much wisdom and humility between these pages that it is hard to come up with an appropriate description. Instead of focusing solely on children's behavior, Israel and Brook direct parents to look deeply at their own reactions to their children. They teach us how to get past our emotional reactions and learn how to respond biblically and model the behavior we want to see in our children. Using their own experiences, including the lapses we all experience, they illustrate how we can tap God's Word to reform ourselves as we learn to gently guide our children to maturity without anger. This book gets my highest recommendation!

**Carolyn Forte, Excellence In Education**

A great blend of straight Bible and straight practical. Israel and Brook live "the real life" with a houseful of kids every day, so their wisdom is tried and tested! As a granddad who yearns to see today's couples turn first to the Word, and second to the experience and wisdom of other godly parents — not the other way around — *Pitchin' A Fit* is a breath of fresh air! Kudos to my good friend Israel and his amazing helpmate, Brook.

**Dale Mason, author, magazine publisher, homeschool dad**

Israel and Brook Wayne offer an excellent treatment for the problem of anger — a problem that afflicts practically every home in the world. This book is surprisingly approachable, highly practical, and biblically fortified throughout.

**Kevin Swanson, pastor, author, host of Generations Radio**

Solid biblical truth and real-life practical help for parents who struggle with whining, screaming, and bad attitudes — and I don't mean the kids!

**Sonya Shafer, founder of Simply Charlotte Mason,**
**author, conference speaker**

Scripture commands fathers to avoid exasperating their children and provoking them to anger. Yet our kid's disobedience seems to naturally bring out the anger buried inside. So how are parents to reach the heart of our young children and shepherd them with grace and gentleness? I'm a firm believer in one of Brook's and Israel's suggestions to "slow down and sit down" when you are suddenly faced with a need to discipline a young one. After all, what's the rush? Slowing down will help you as much as it will bless your children. Give it a try. I bet you will feel better about the whole process.

**Davis Carman, President, Apologia Educational Ministries**

In their new book, *Pitchin' a Fit*, Israel and Brook Wayne provide us with a deeply comprehensive look at anger, both in our personal lives and in the family context: What are the origins of anger? Is anger ever justified? What does Scripture mean by not provoking our children to anger? How can parents deal with anger among siblings? With anger at their own children? Much more. Israel is a gifted, and much sought-after speaker on the subject of family and parenting issues. I recommend this book for every parent, even those who don't think they have anger issues. You will be helped by the insights Israel and Brook share on these pages!

**Chris Davis, Author, conference speaker, publisher**

What a welcome breath of fresh air in a very me-focused culture to find a book willing to tackle what I believe is a real problem for Christian parents. Israel and Brook Wayne share their struggles while going one step further than most books, giving practical advice that will actually work. Not only do they give you advice on getting to the root of the problem, but enclosed is a roadmap to freedom, as well. If you need a book that will help you conquer anger and deal with stress with a big dose of encouragement, I highly recommend this book.

**Felice Gerwitz, author and podcaster,**
**founder of Media Angels, Inc.**

OVERCOMING ANGRY *and*
STRESSED-OUT PARENTING

# PITCHIN' A FIT!

## Israel & Brook Wayne

First printing: March 2016
Third printing: September 2019

New Leaf Press, P.O. Box 726, Green Forest, AR 72638
New Leaf Press is a division of the New Leaf Publishing Group, Inc.

ISBN: 978-0-89221-739-7
ISBN: 978-1-61458-484-1 (digital)
Library of Congress Number: 2016931405

Cover by Left Coast Design, Portland Oregon

Unless otherwise noted, Scripture quotations are from the English
Standard Version (ESV) of the Bible.

Please consider requesting that a copy of this volume be purchased
by your local library system.

**Printed in the United States of America**

Please visit our website for other great titles:
www.newleafpress.com

For information regarding author interviews,
please contact the publicity department at (870) 438-5288.

**New Leaf Press**
A Division of New Leaf Publishing Group
www.newleafpress.com

All your children shall be taught by the Lord, and great shall be the peace of your children (Isa. 54:13).

**Dedicated to** our precious children, each of whom has enriched our lives in countless ways. Our prayer for each of you is that you will look to the Lord all the days of your life and allow Him to lead you. May great peace follow you all the days of your life. We love you more than life itself.

And to the parents walking this journey with us, looking to put off the weight of our own weaknesses and faults for the sake of seeing God work in each of our children.

**Special Thanks** to Sony Elise for her editing skills, time, and love. You are a great sister, and we're thankful to co-labor with you.

**Special Thanks** to Tim Dudley for believing in us! Thank you to the whole team at New Leaf Publishing Group for your dedication and hard work to produce "ink on paper to touch eternity."

# Contents

# Introduction

*Israel:* It was a simple request. "Make sure you feed the chickens before we leave." That's not exactly rocket science. However, when you give an instruction to a child, you never know how things may turn out.

We were all loaded up in our 15-passenger van, ready for our 31-day road trip across America. As a public speaker I travel frequently, speaking at churches, conferences, retreats, seminars, camps, and other events on a variety of Christian-living topics. The nice thing about not being tied to a "day job" is that I sometimes get to take my whole family with me. My wife, my sister, and our flock of children were waiting on me as I locked our house and proceeded to the vehicle.

As I was getting into the van, I noticed a sight that sent a shock of emotions pulsing through my system all at once. In front of our closed garage door were about 25 chickens, all ravenously trying to push the others aside so they could single-handedly consume the 50-pound bag of feed that had been dumped there.

"What in the world!" I exclaimed as I walked over for closer inspection. My mind was having a hard time taking this in. I could feel the frustration rising. I walked over to our van, opened the door, and instructed the child in question to accompany me to the crime scene.

"What did I tell you to do?" I asked sternly.

"Feed the chickens."

"Right. So why did you do this?"

"I fed them."

"This is NOT the way you feed the chickens!" (My blood pressure was rising.)

(Silence.)

"You know that I wanted you to take the feed to the chicken coop, which is 150 yards from here in the *BACK YARD*! In what universe do you think THIS is okay?"

"You didn't say *where* to feed them. You just said to feed them."

"Seriously? Are we really having this conversation? Why didn't you leave them in the chicken coop? Did it not occur to you that we would be leaving for 31 DAYS? Did you not consider that since your aunt is coming to feed them for us, she will NOT want the responsibility of chasing 25 chickens around the yard and catching them? And WHAT could have possibly convinced you that right in front of our garage door was a location where I would want chickens pooping all over the place? What on earth were you thinking?"

"I don't know."

"You don't know?" Yep. I was angry. "Get in the van!"

The child quickly retreated to the van (which was still running), while I began to think of what to do. I knew that chickens have the ability to eat almost constantly, so there was very little threat of the feed still being there by the end of the day. I knew this would require my (other) sister to buy more feed while we were gone (which I hated to have her do). I knew that we would get a late start if we took time to capture the chickens, but if we didn't, my sister would have that unpleasant task.

Most of all, I knew I had just done what I have always told my children not to do. I lost my temper. Now when I say I "lost it," I don't mean that I lost it in any kind of seriously out-of-control way. No one in the situation was in fear for his or her safety. But I had raised my voice and I had spoken in anger. I hated that.

I noticed that my wife and sister were watching me pace back in forth in the driveway, muttering to myself. I needed to cool down. The problem was that every time I glanced toward the garage, the emotions all flooded back.

Finally, I walked toward the van, climbed in, and sat down. I was about to put the vehicle in drive when I remembered our family's tradition. Before we leave on a long trip, we pray for safety and blessing. I thought about the purpose of this trip. We were going to meet with thousands of families across America who were hurting and needed help and encouragement. I always ask my children after our time of prayer, "Why are we going on this trip?" They all respond, "To bless people!"

There was *no way* I was fit to be a blessing to anyone at that moment. In fact, I felt rather hypocritical about even praying. I was pretty sure that God wouldn't be interested in hearing anything I had to say. Or worse yet, He probably already had heard everything I had just said (and how I said it). I looked in the rearview mirror, made eye contact with the offending child, and said, "Get out of the van."

We both stepped outside, and I took five deep breaths. I looked up toward the sky, said a silent prayer for help and grace, and then repented to my child.

"I was wrong. That was not an acceptable way for me to respond to you. Now let me be very clear . . . what you did was not acceptable either . . . but that does not excuse me. I spoke to you in anger, and that is not what I want to do."

"That's okay," came the quick reply. (Children are so eager to forgive, even when their parents have been out of line.)

"I appreciate that you forgive me, but no, it's not okay, and I don't want you to ever think that it is. By God's grace I want to respond more appropriately in the future. I will be praying about this and asking God to change my heart. Will you pray for me as well?"

"Sure."

"Okay, I love you."

"Thanks. I love you too."

"Are you ready to go?

"I think so."

"Okay, let's see if we can have a better trip now. Oh, but first, we need to catch some chickens and clean up a mess."

I wish I could say that this was the only such scenario in my many years of parenting. It was not. However, I am thankful that, for all of my failures as a father, God has continued to teach me His ways and help me to mature. Those moments for me are relatively infrequent and are not life defining.

### Taming the Meanie Monster

If you are a parent, you have been there. Children do things that test the limits of those of us who admire rationality and common sense. Our innate default in such moments is to respond badly. We all struggle with anger to some extent. It is only through learning what God has to say on the subject of anger, and through appropriating the power of the Holy Spirit, that we can escape the tyranny of our own tendencies and addictions.

If you struggle with habitual anger, there are several things you need to know.

1.  You are not alone. Everyone struggles with this issue to some extent.
2.  It is not okay. Left unchecked it will damage important relationships.
3.  There is hope. There is freedom found in God's Word to help you overcome this habitual sin.

We hope that you will join us on a mission to escape the trap of angry and stressed-out parenting. In this book, we will share with you a biblical view of anger, strategies for breaking life-long habits, and ways that you can build up and encourage your child rather than tear him or her down.

We believe that there is life-transforming power in the truth of Scripture, and we know that better days are in store for you and your family through God's grace.

# 1

# Stressed Out and Overwhelmed

*Brook:* It was Sunday morning. We were running late
. . . again. I detest being late. I get it from my dad, who
is punctual on the side of early. Nothing had gone right
that morning. The oatmeal had burned right under my
nose as I put the finishing touches on our crockpot dish
to share for lunch. We had been out the night before, so
there were too many people waiting in line for a shower
and, way too early, the hot water was exhausted. The
girls couldn't find their tights, one of the boys' shirts had
a stain on it. We finally dashed out the door. During the
drive, my mind was still in a muddled mess about all
the little imperfections we had left behind, as well as the
ones that went with us. Ugh! One of the girls' tights had
a hole in it! Why hadn't I noticed that! I was sure everyone else would notice it! And the perfectly combed hair
of several children was all askew as they had tussled
with each other to get out the door. Then there were
the breakfast dishes left on the table. Why couldn't we
get it together to at least get them to the sink? Just as I
was feeling out of sorts, wouldn't you know it, we took a
turn, and, well, the crockpot. . . .

As we finally resolved the crockpot situation, I actually took the time to count up each of the irritations I
had faced that morning. Every last little irksome, imperfect dent on my day. No one item was large or significant
in and of itself. Nevertheless, I felt like a tremendous
failure. Just why do little stressors have to all gang up on
me together, and in the morning to boot?

As I faced out the window, ignoring the children's
chatter, I had to admit to myself that there really wasn't
all that much to get worked up about. With some better
pre-planning, many of those little problems could be
avoided. But what stared back at me from the vehicle's
window was the fact that I had come to love so much

having all my "ducks in a row," everything organized and "just so," that I was willing to get all bent out of shape when "perfect" didn't happen. I had to ask myself, "Did Jesus suffer, die on the cross, and rise again, so I could have a flawless, organized, picture-perfect life with no bumps?"

By taking on stress in a million small ways, I had allowed stress to narrow my vision to a very small world — one where I got to be in command. Jesus came to bring salvation to a vast world of sinners caught in the chains of addiction to self. And here I was, all in an emotional despair, because one of my children didn't wear his good shoes and didn't comb his hair?

Sure, there can be quite a bit of benefit to examining how to streamline family life and its various functions, but feeling out of sorts doesn't help accomplish that. My heart's focus had gotten off the riches and fullness of Christ and had settled onto the temporary. And, for many of us, that's where we open the door for stress to come in and roost.

### The Illusion of the Life of Ease

None of us likes trials, big or small. We like to safeguard our lives and avoid stress at all costs. We like to have everything pristine and under control. Some of us work very hard at not taking on more than we can handle. But life isn't always like that. It throws us curveballs and bumps and losses when we least expect it. We can't hide in an ivory tower. If we try, we end up shutting *people* out of our lives. Parenting, in particular, brings its own set of stresses related to the care and upbringing of children. The bills, the broken legs, the cobwebs, the repairs, the dishes — they can all look so big and scary, and seek to knock us off course!

If, instead, we keep our eyes on the Lord, trusting He has a plan through all of this, a load will be lifted from our shoulders.

The Lord tells us that His burden is light. He will give grace in the day we need it.

### Stress Can Lead to Anger

Not surprisingly, stress can be hugely detrimental to health. Every year, experts reveal the negative effects stress brings about on our physical bodies, emotions, and spiritual well-being. Furthermore, stress can get into our homes and affect the family.

We want to point out that stress and anger are not always cut out of the same cloth. Many stressed-out parents are not necessarily angry parents. However, stress is often a trigger point for anger. Stressed-out (but not angry) parents can bring a different tension to the home than angry parents, but it is still not a healthy atmosphere.

### Anger Exists on a Spectrum

Suppose we charted anger on a kind of timeline, from left to right. On the far left, we'd find very mild expressions of anger, moving toward more advanced stages on the right: impatience, irritation, annoyance, edginess, frustration, agitation, exasperation, anger, fury, wrath, frenzy, hatred, and rage.

Most of us, as Christians, are pretty aware that the expressions on the far right are unacceptable for God's people. However, too often we give ourselves a free pass on the lighter expressions of anger, feeling like they aren't all that bad. The problem is that in most cases, anger, like cancer, isn't good for us. It's really not something we want to have affixed to our person, because it usually grows and metastasizes.

### Stress Tends to Lead to Fear

Let's face it — most of us lead some pretty busy lives. It's a lot to keep up with family life, work, household maintenance, etc. In the face of deadlines, repairs, obligations, and responsibilities, the panic of whether we can pull it all off stems from fear. We're afraid we won't get everything on our to-do list done on time.

We're afraid that we'll mess up some major job by not getting the details correct. Maybe we're even so overbooked that we feel stress that we're not working on one task because another task has tied us up!

Stress in parenting can also stem from fear. We're afraid we'll ruin our poor kids. Or maybe we're a little fearful we won't be all we ought to be as moms and dads. We're afraid that they'll grow up to resent us for not getting them that puppy, or new bike, or the latest technology. That's nothing to say of the near accidents we save our children from throughout their childhood. The fear and stress a climbing toddler can give his parents is akin to teaching a teenager how to drive.

Yet, while we live with all of these challenges (and I'm sure you could think of many more), fear is not something that God intends for us. While we're on this earth, we're going to have trouble. Thanks to our great-great-plus-granddaddy Adam, we're fighting those thistles with the sweat of our brow, working hard to bring children into the world. Even through all the struggles we face in our modern lives, God's intent is that we don't live by a spirit of fear.

> **Brook:** These precious words Paul wrote to Timothy have stuck out to me: "I am reminded of your sincere *faith*, a faith that dwelt first in your grandmother Lois and your mother Eunice and now, I am sure, dwells in you as well. For this reason I remind you to *fan into flame* the gift of God, which is in you through the laying on of my hands, for God gave us a spirit *not of fear* but of power and love and self-control" (2 Tim. 1:5–7, emphasis added).
>
> Allow me to slip in a substitute word for a minute: "For God gave us a spirit not of [being overwhelmed]." I know it says "fear," but think with me, what is being overwhelmed? It is fear that we can't keep up or live up

to our calling — fear that we can't raise our children properly.

### Stir up God's Gifts

A spirit of fear is not a gift of God. This is not the gift 2 Timothy is indicating we're supposed to fan into flames. When we give into stress by living and feeding off of it, we're stirring it up. We stir it up by dwelling on our stress, feeling pity for ourselves, and rehearsing in the privacy of our minds how we're really being imposed upon.

There is no shame in feeling stressed. It is likely going to happen to each and every one of us along the days of our parenting, and probably many times. However, living in a continual state of being overwhelmed is a choice. Webster's 1828 Dictionary defines overwhelm: "To overspread or crush beneath something violent and weighty, that covers or encompasses the whole, as to overwhelm with waves. To immerse and bear down; in a figurative sense; as, to be overwhelmed with cares, afflictions, or business."[1]

There is such a spirit of passivity in the very word "overwhelmed." A feeling is only a feeling. A feeling only becomes part of you when you allow it to take up residence. Next time you begin to feel stressed, you won't "feel" like remembering the gifts God has placed in you, much less exerting the effort to stir up that gift, so you need to prepare yourself beforehand. Ask yourself questions such as: "What am I going to do when I feel stressed out? How can I prevent my feelings from controlling how I interact with my children?"

Take a look at what God gives you:

### A Spirit of Power

God provides His power to enable you to raise your children. He won't call you to anything for which He will not equip you. When God calls us to a responsibility or an area of service, He will provide His strength and resources. Avail yourself of what He offers!

---

1. http://av1611.com/kjbp/kjv-dictionary/overwhelm.html.

"Now may the God of peace who brought again from the dead our Lord Jesus, the great shepherd of the sheep, by the blood of the eternal covenant, equip you with everything good that you may do his will, working in us that which is pleasing in his sight, through Jesus Christ, to whom be glory forever and ever. Amen" (Heb. 13:20–21).

When stress is overtaking you, whether directly with your youngsters or through the stresses of life, call on the power of God to provide you with direction.

> **Brook:** Not long ago, I became aware of a large home repair we needed to make. The whole thing stressed me out right from the beginning. It was something outside of my skill set. I didn't know how to go about fixing it. I knew it would be costly, and all that stress came out in my relationships with my family. After snapping at everyone for about the third time, I realized that I had better get some prayer time in . . . and quickly! I took the stressful repair to the Lord, acknowledged my wrong in allowing it to interfere in my family, and simply asked for help.
>
> Throughout the next day, every time I thought of that repair, my heart raced a little faster. But I reminded myself that I had a choice to make: was I going to allow my stress to affect my family? I had prayed about the issue and was calmly looking into how to go about that repair. My adding panic to the situation wasn't going to make things better! This is the power of God in us, to say no to ungodly behavior and turn from it, however many times a day it is necessary.

### A Spirit of Love

When we feel overwhelmed, we feel depleted, and about the last thing we want to do is invest in our families, yet cultivating a spirit of love produces in us a deep-rooted realization that people are more important than things. Relationships are never worth losing over stress. Stir up this gift by allowing God's love to flow through you to your family.

When we feel stressed, we're often in a hurry because of the clock. It is easy to be a slave to our calendar. Fear wants to hold us down and shut off the flow of love within us. But fear isn't the spirit God wants to see expressed in our homes. Even through tough times, the rare beauty of love is what will carry us through.

> *Brook:* I'm reminded of a dear, kind mom, Kelli, who struggled with a vicious form of cancer while her children were yet young. As soon as she learned of the cancer, fear (naturally) gripped her heart and expressed itself every chance it got. She found, as her condition worsened, that the fear had altered her home. No longer did she talk kindly to her children. Life had become one long session of pain and tension. Yet, as death stared her in the face, she knew this wasn't the legacy she wanted to leave behind should this be the end of her earthly story. Slowly, purposefully, she sought to replace the fear that terrorized her day and night, with love. Wherever she could sprinkle love, she did it. When she talked about her hope to live, she put in a dose of why she loved her family so much. When she shared about her pain, she thanked her family for their love for her, and reminded them of her love for them. Kelli's time was not long, and as I have heard about it, her farewell was filled with an intense expression of love. Her choice in the midst of the ultimate stress was profound.

### A Spirit of Self-Control

Other translations refer to this alternately as "self-discipline" or "sound mind," which I think is very fitting. Quite possibly, you will go through some time in your parenting when you feel like you are losing your mind. Those feelings are not meant to become the fabric with which you parent. The phrase "self-discipline" also provides such rich treasure for parenting. If we, moms and dads, walk in self-discipline, even just in the practical aspects of our lives, we are taking a huge swipe at minimizing stress.

Stress can sometimes bring with it a sense of entitlement. We may feel like we are working long hours, whether in a job or in the home, and not getting enough recognition. When we feel put out about the weight of stress we carry around, we open the door for that stress to come out on others (our families mainly) for not helping out in the way we think they should. So we bark at them and feel justified. Or we holler and snap angrily back. Or we make unreasonable demands and put each other down. In our attempts to gain some kind of control over the chaos life sometimes throws at us, we threaten and connive and give up *self*-control. When we do so, we are letting stress have control, and it is not a good or kind master. Panic becomes its sidekick, and you are led around in its grip.

God is in the business of turning us worn-out, tired, stressed, and even *angry* parents into ones filled with self-control.

### Work and Stress

**Brook:** Many times stress is directly related to the pressures to accomplish a certain job by a given time. After speaking about stressed and angry parenting, I had some time to sit down with a mom who works from home about four hours each afternoon. Her three children range in age from 7 to 11, and she was pulling her hair out trying to keep an eye on her children and fulfill the pressing duties in front of her.

"Basically," she began, "I feel like I am under so much stress just running from my desk to break up squabbles and fix problems, and trying to act as judge, and then heading back to my desk and trying to remember where I was. We need the money from my job, but

I can't handle the stress! And I know I'm sharp with the kids because of it. Can you give me some advice?"

I encouraged her (if possible) to take one afternoon off of work and focus solely on coming up with a game plan for her children. Over the years, I have found that children who are given clear instructions on what they are "supposed" to be doing are much easier to manage than children left to their own creative and mischievous devices. I mentioned that she might even want to include her children in giving her a few of their suggestions.

Here's what I suggested for coming up with a definitive plan:

1. Break up your work afternoon into slots about 30–45 minutes long, switching from something fun and hands-on, to something more quiet and studious in rotation every change of time slot.
2. Talk to your children about the new setup, and try it out for an afternoon or more to fix any glitches. Then paste it where the children can see. Now, for the next two weeks, you can't expect that it will go well. Your job during this time is to realize you may still have just as many interruptions, but, each time, you will have something solid and concrete to turn your children back toward.
3. At the end of those two weeks, with consistency, you should begin to start seeing progress.

Stress is often brought about by the tension we feel when we have too many priorities at one time. It can also come through procrastination or the tension between working and relaxing. Working toward utilizing our time in a self-disciplined way can go a long way toward reducing stress.

Stress often leads to disappointment. We want things to go a certain way, and tension builds when it doesn't. Pain and irritation can also lead to anger and stress.

### The Three-Ring Circus

There have been a few times (maybe more!) where I think I have reached the point that parenting has fully equipped me to capably handle running a three-ring circus. I remember when our second child was born and I felt like my mind was going to split in two taking care of an active toddler *and* a tiny infant. God has since gifted us with a houseful of children (nine at the time of this writing), and there are days I shake my head, while the baby needs attention, the soup boils over, Cubbie wants to learn to tie his shoes, Teddy Bear wants help learning his fractions, my oldest explores various career choices, and my butterfly girl dances and dreams and flits from one project to the next. Like all of you, the daily stresses of family life, a business to run, bills to pay, and unfinished projects mount, and we have a choice: how are we going to handle the various needs and tensions pulling on us? We can let stress overtake us. Or we can look for ways to employ the power of God, love, and self-control in the *midst* of all that stress.

### Saying No to Outside Extras

One of the mantras we often hear from time-management experts is the need to say no to some things in order to say yes to the very best. If stress has come to live in your home, take serious inventory as a couple and as a family of ways you can reduce your activities.

### And When You Can't Say No

But we also recognize there are all sorts of times that saying no to responsibilities is simply not an option. In these times, look for ways to double utilize the time by building with your family. Do you have work-related responsibilities that allow for the whole family to be together? Or are you able, as a family, to reach out to a family in need? Deuteronomy 6 provides rich instruction for finding time to bond with our families around the Lord, even during the busyness of life.

### Searching for Some Margin

As parents, we may need to redefine what margin and refreshment look like. Parents don't really have the luxury of taking a lot of personal time, a common go-to for many folks for relaxation. Nevertheless, moms and dads need times to be rejuvenated, and creatively finding rest in the midst of family life is a must. Maybe it looks less like a round of golf, a visit to the local shopping center, or a quiet weekend getaway, and more like huge bowls of popcorn, reading aloud together, or sitting quietly on a park bench while little ones run off some energy. Rest and refueling in the family setting are different, but some of it comes down to snatching quiet and refreshing moments, as they come, with thankfulness. There will come a day when we'll have all kinds of time to ourselves for non-family-related pursuits. I hear from empty nesters that they miss these busy days we find ourselves in.

Margin for moms and dads is possible, just different. It might come in snatching an opportunity to spend one-on-one time as a couple or with one of the children, or in sitting for a few moments on the porch with a cup of hot coffee. We all need space, even our active and social teenagers, and energetic toddlers. Taking "down time" as a regular routine can have huge benefits for keeping sanity for the whole family. Guard your calendar carefully so that you don't entirely squeeze out margin in your life.

When even your carefully planned and trimmed life seems relentless, remember this season of parenting is a stretching season for everyone. If you feel like stretched-out elastic, take heart, because it means you are being stretched to hold more of God.

### Feeding on the Real Deal

Just as doughnuts and candy give a false sense of fullness without delivering nutrition, it is important to make sure we are spiritually and emotionally refueling on that which will really give us refreshment. There is no problem with pampering sorts of relaxation if that fits in with your lifestyle, but don't miss out on getting the real food of the Word of God deep into your existence in order to be fed. Ultimately, God's Word is going to be the real source of strength as we walk through parenting.

### Questions to Consider

What are the three biggest areas of stress for you right now? Are there any ways in which you see stress affecting your family?

What are two ways you could make a few minutes of margin this week? What are two ways that you could find some rest and relaxation with your family?

What do you see the benefits could be of responding to stress with prayer (calling on the power of God), love, and self-discipline?

# 2

# Is It Wrong to Get Angry?

Oftentimes, people defend anger using Scripture. The Bible frequently mentions the need to be slow to anger, but is it forbidden altogether? God gets angry, right? Didn't Jesus get angry? Why shouldn't we? Let's examine what the Bible has to say about this topic. (You may want to refer back to this chapter as needed as a source for further study and Scripture memorization on this topic.)

### Be Slow to Get Angry

A man of quick temper acts foolishly ... (Prov. 14:17).

Whoever is slow to anger has great understanding, but he who has a hasty temper exalts folly (Prov. 14:29).

A hot-tempered man stirs up strife, but he who is slow to anger quiets contention (Prov. 15:18).

Whoever is slow to anger is better than the mighty, and he who rules his spirit than he who takes a city (Prov. 16:32).

Good sense makes one slow to anger, and it is his glory to overlook an offense (Prov. 19:11).

Be not quick in your spirit to become angry, for anger lodges in the heart of fools (Eccles. 7:9).

All of these Scriptures warn against hasty anger, but none of them condemn anger altogether.

In Titus 1:7–8, we are told that church elders must not be quick-tempered, but instead must be self-controlled and disciplined.

So it is quite clear from these passages that someone who "flies off the handle" readily is going against the weight of Scripture.

### Is Anger Permissible at All?

There are only a few places in the Bible where anger seems to be given any allowance at all, and each of these places attaches a strong warning label to the idea.

> Be angry, and do not sin; ponder in your own hearts on your beds, and be silent. Selah. Offer right sacrifices, and put your trust in the LORD (Ps. 4:4–5).

> Be angry and do not sin; do not let the sun go down on your anger, and give no opportunity to the devil (Eph. 4:26–27).

However, just a few verses later we read:

> Let *all* bitterness and wrath and anger and clamor and slander be put away from you, along with all malice. Be kind to one another, tenderhearted, forgiving one another, as God in Christ forgave you (Eph. 4:31–32, emphasis added).

We are also instructed:

> But now you must put them *all* away: anger, wrath, malice, slander, and obscene talk from your mouth (Col. 3:8, emphasis added).

> Refrain from anger, and forsake wrath! Fret not yourself; it tends only to evil. For the evildoers shall be cut off, but those who wait for the LORD shall inherit the land (Ps. 37:8–9).

First Corinthians 13:5 tells us that love is not irritable. Proverbs 27:4 reminds us: "Wrath is cruel, anger is overwhelming." We are even warned that anger can be contagious.

> Make no friendship with a man given to anger, nor go with a wrathful man, lest you learn his ways and entangle yourself in a snare (Prov. 22:24–25).

### God's Anger

It is frequently argued, "God gets angry, and Jesus got angry in the temple, so why can't I get angry?"

> God *is* a just judge, and God is angry *with the wicked* every day (Ps. 7:11, NKJV, italics original).

> For the wrath of God is revealed from heaven against all ungodliness and unrighteousness of men, who by their unrighteousness suppress the truth (Rom. 1:18).

The Bible tells us that God gets angry; however, in His infinite holiness, He does not sin in the application of His anger. We must always remember that God's anger is an expression of His divine love, holiness, and justice. We also are told that God does not get angry quickly or act hastily in His righteous judgment.

> The LORD, the LORD, a God merciful and gracious, slow to anger, and abounding in steadfast love and faithfulness" (Exod. 34:6).

> Yet he, being compassionate, atoned for their iniquity and did not destroy them; he restrained his anger often and did not stir up all his wrath. He remembered that they were but flesh, a wind that passes and comes not again (Ps. 78:38–39).

> The LORD is merciful and gracious, slow to anger and abounding in steadfast love. He will not always chide, nor will he keep his anger forever. He does not deal with us according to our sins, nor repay us according to our iniquities. For as high as the heavens are above the earth, so great is his steadfast love toward those who fear him; as far as the east is from the west, so far does he remove our transgressions from us. As a father shows compassion to his children, so the

Lord shows compassion to those who fear him. For he knows our frame; he remembers that we are dust (Ps. 103:8–14).

For my name's sake I defer my anger, for the sake of my praise I restrain it for you, that I may not cut you off (Isa. 48:9).

The Lord is not slow to fulfill his promise as some count slowness, but is patient toward you, not wishing that any should perish, but that all should reach repentance (2 Pet. 3:9).

God's love is always in perfect balance with His justice. So whatever God does is always what is best for humankind, even though it is often difficult for us to understand His ways.

### Jesus' Anger

Again he entered the synagogue, and a man was there with a withered hand. And they watched Jesus, to see whether he would heal him on the Sabbath, so that they might accuse him. And he said to the man with the withered hand, "Come here." And he said to them, "Is it lawful on the Sabbath to do good or to do harm, to save life or to kill?" But they were silent. And *he looked around at them with anger*, grieved at their hardness of heart, and said to the man, "Stretch out your hand." He stretched it out, and his hand was restored (Mark 3:1–5, emphasis added).

And they were bringing children to him that he might touch them, and the disciples rebuked them. But when Jesus saw it, *he was indignant* and said to them, "Let the children come to me; do not hinder them, for to such belongs the kingdom of God" (Mark 10:13–14, emphasis added).

Some people will point to Jesus driving out the moneychangers in the temple as an example of His anger, or perhaps even rage. However, given the context, we see that Jesus actually took time to weave His own whip. He wasn't in a hurry or rage. Also, it seems most likely that this cleansing of the temple happened twice.

> Jesus cleansed the temple on at least two occasions. The first time was near the beginning of His ministry, as described in John. The final time was just prior to His death, as described in the Synoptics.[1]

So while Jesus was certainly motivated by a righteous indignation against the misuse of His Father's house, I think the idea that He flew into a rage on the spur of the moment and acted hastily and impulsively is out of the question here.

What we do know is that Jesus' anger was always stirred by injustice, and His actions when angry were always on behalf of the oppressed, or for the honor of the Father, and never in His own self-defense. In fact, during His trial, He remained silent in the face of His accusers (demonstrating amazing restraint and self-control).

> When he was reviled, he did not revile in return; when he suffered, he did not threaten, but continued entrusting himself to him who judges justly (1 Pet. 2:23).

We may gain an insight from the Apostle John on this: "His disciples remembered that it was written, 'Zeal for your house will consume me' " (John 2:17). It is clear that Jesus was zealous, but that is a different thing than senseless rage. Jesus was motivated by zeal for a righteous cause.

### Judgment for Anger

We are told in Scripture that there can even be eternal consequences to our human anger.

---

1. Tim Chaffey, *Demolishing Supposed Bible Contradictions* (Green Forest, AR: Master Books, 2012), p. 130; https://answersingenesis.org/jesus-christ/when-did-jesus-cleanse-the-temple.

You have heard that it was said to those of old, "You shall not murder; and whoever murders will be liable to judgment." But I say to you that *everyone who is angry with his brother will be liable to judgment*; whoever insults his brother will be liable to the council; and *whoever says, "You fool!" will be liable to the hell of fire.* So if you are offering your gift at the altar and there remember that your brother has something against you, leave your gift there before the altar and go. First be reconciled to your brother, and then come and offer your gift (Matt. 5:21–24, emphasis added).

Do not speak evil against one another, brothers. The one who speaks against a brother or judges his brother, speaks evil against the law and judges the law. But if you judge the law, you are not a doer of the law but a judge. There is only one lawgiver and judge, he who is able to save and to destroy. But who are you to judge your neighbor? (James 4:11–12).

So why the double standard? Why is it okay for God to get angry, but not us?

### Anger Will Not Produce the Desired Result

Know this, my beloved brothers: let every person be quick to hear, slow to speak, slow to anger; for the anger of man does not produce the righteousness of God (James 1:19–20).

While on the one hand James seems to legitimize anger by reminding us to be slow about it, he then turns around and tells us that it will not achieve for us the end result we are hoping for. This is the principle of sowing and reaping. We cannot sow seeds of anger in our child's life and expect to reap a harvest of God's righteousness. If you sow a corn kernel, you cannot justly expect an apple tree to grow there. It's not the right kind of DNA. In the same way, if you consistently, as a lifestyle, respond in anger to your children, the fruit you can expect will be anger, bitterness, and resentment from your child.

### Flesh or Spirit?

> Now the deeds of the flesh are evident, which are: immorality, impurity, sensuality, idolatry, sorcery, enmities, strife, jealousy, outbursts of anger, disputes, dissensions, factions, envying, drunkenness, carousing, and things like these, of which I forewarn you, just as I have forewarned you, that those who practice such things will not inherit the kingdom of God. But the fruit of the Spirit is love, joy, peace, patience, kindness, goodness, faithfulness, gentleness, self-control; against such things there is no law. Now those who belong to Christ Jesus have crucified the flesh with its passions and desires (Gal. 5:19–24; NASB).

Because human anger in relationships is so often defended by Christians, it may actually surprise us to discover that anger is a work of our own flesh, and not something righteous that God is producing in us. Our natural, fleshly instinct is to respond in an angry manner to people. We don't need to be taught this reflex. We inherited it at birth. At the same time, learning to master this tendency to respond angrily toward others is a work of God's Holy Spirit inside of us. Self-control is God's solution to our tendency toward angry outbursts.

### Self-Control

I don't believe the impulse of anger is a sin. However, our expression of it, through words and actions, usually are. Instead of giving vent to our anger, we are encouraged to demonstrate self-control.

> The vexation of a fool is known at once, but the prudent ignores an insult (Prov. 12:16).

A soft answer turns away wrath, but a harsh word stirs up anger (Prov. 15:1).

A man without self-control is like a city broken into and left without walls (Prov. 25:28).

A fool gives full vent to his spirit, but a wise man quietly holds it back (Prov. 29:11).

A man of wrath stirs up strife, and one given to anger causes much transgression (Prov. 29:22).

Bearing with one another and, if one has a complaint against another, forgiving each other; as the LORD has forgiven you, so you also must forgive (Col. 3:13).

### Righteous Indignation

A time to love, and a time to hate; a time for war, and a time for peace (Eccles. 3:8).

How can there be a time to hate if hatred is always a sinful, wrong emotion? The fact is, there is an appropriate expression of anger for the Christian. The emotion of anger (and appropriate actions resulting from it) are not only allowable, but commendable, when they are expressed against human injustice on behalf of the oppressed, or when God's honor is mocked by the ungodly.

In Exodus 11:8, Moses became angry when Pharaoh refused to listen to God's command and hardened his heart against God and His people. This was not anger from being personally offended or insulted (as was the case in Numbers 20:11, when Moses struck the rock in disregard for God's Word, and was disciplined by not getting to enter the Promised Land). We see that Moses had both the capacity for godly anger, directed appropriately, and unrestrained human anger exerted on his own behalf.

In Exodus 32, Moses descended from the mountain of God with the stone tablets of the law in his hands. When he heard the yells from the Israelites as they indulged in pagan revelry around the golden calf they had made, he became very angry and broke the tablets of stone (and dished out some retribution on those involved). He was zealous for the holiness of God.

In 1 Samuel 17, young David was righteously indignant when he heard the Philistine warrior, Goliath, mocking the armies of the living God. Something stirred within him that something needed to be done.

Righteous Job declared of himself and his actions:

> I delivered the poor who cried for help, and the fatherless who had none to help him. The blessing of him who was about to perish came upon me, and I caused the widow's heart to sing for joy. I put on righteousness, and it clothed me; my justice was like a robe and a turban. I was eyes to the blind and feet to the lame. I was a father to the needy, and I searched out the cause of him whom I did not know. I broke the fangs of the unrighteous and made him drop his prey from his teeth (Job 29:12–17).

Lot also experienced this anger:

> Lot [was] greatly distressed by the sensual conduct of the wicked ("for as that righteous man lived among them day after day, he was tormenting his righteous soul over their lawless deeds that he saw and heard) (2 Pet. 2:7–8).

True righteous indignation is always for the cause of the oppressed, righteousness, or the honor of God, and never on our own self-serving behalf.

### A Cry to God for Justice

The Bible gives us many commendable narratives of people who expressed anger and appropriate actions against evil and injustice. In the Psalms and prophetic books, we see many prayers and laments that deal with not only evil in the outside world, but anger against personal offense as well. Expressing anger to God regarding sins and injustices committed against us is the proper expression and direction of our feelings of anger.

> Arise, O LORD! Save me, O my God! For you strike all my enemies on the cheek; you break the teeth of the wicked (Ps. 3:7).

> Arise, O LORD, in your anger; lift yourself up against the fury of my enemies; awake for me; you have appointed a judgment (Ps. 7:6).

> O LORD, God of vengeance, O God of vengeance, shine forth! Rise up, O judge of the earth; repay to the proud what they deserve! O LORD, how long shall the wicked, how long shall the wicked exult? (Ps. 94:1–3).

> Oh that you would slay the wicked, O God! O men of blood, depart from me! They speak against you with malicious intent; your enemies take your name in vain. Do I not hate those who hate you, O LORD? And do I not loathe those who rise up against you? I hate them with complete hatred; I count them my enemies (Ps. 139:19–22).

> O LORD, how long shall I cry for help, and you will not hear? Or cry to you "Violence!" and you will not save? Why do you make me see iniquity, and why do you idly look at wrong? Destruction and violence are before me; strife and contention arise. So the law is paralyzed, and justice never goes forth. For the wicked surround the righteous; so justice goes forth perverted (Hab. 1:2–4).

Even in the afterlife, there are those who cry to God for justice.

When he opened the fifth seal, I saw under the altar the souls of those who had been slain for the word of God and for the witness they had borne. They cried out with a loud voice, "O Sovereign Lord, holy and true, how long before you will judge and avenge our blood on those who dwell on the earth?" Then they were each given a white robe and told to rest a little longer, until the number of their fellow servants and their brothers should be complete, who were to be killed as they themselves had been (Rev. 6:9–11).

## God Will Repay

The fact is, we have very clear instructions in the Bible about how we should deal with personal injustice against us. We are to leave final judgment in the hands of God. Even if, for the perpetrator's own sake, or for the sake of protecting others, we seek justice through human courts, ultimately, God will avenge.

You shall not hate your brother in your heart, but you shall reason frankly with your neighbor, lest you incur sin because of him. You shall not take vengeance or bear a grudge against the sons of your own people, but you shall love your neighbor as yourself: I am the Lord (Lev. 19:17–18).

"Vengeance is mine, and recompense, for the time when their foot shall slip; for the day of their calamity is at hand, and their doom comes swiftly." For the Lord will vindicate his people and have compassion on his servants (Deut. 32:35–36).

Repay no one evil for evil, but give thought to do what is honorable in the sight of all. If possible, so far as it depends on you, live peaceably with all. Beloved, never avenge yourselves, but leave it to the wrath of

God, for it is written, "Vengeance is mine, I will repay, says the Lord" (Rom. 12:17–19).

### Understanding Our Anger

Because we are made in the image of God, we have many of His communicable attributes. God feels and expresses anger, and so do we. However, unlike God, we do not possess infinite wisdom, infinite love, and infinite holiness. So anger in our lives must be handled with extreme caution. We must not think that we can use anger in our own defense without the strong likelihood of crossing into sin. God has warned us repeatedly about the dangers of anger. It is appropriate to feel, and properly express, anger when we see genuine sin and injustice, but we must ensure that we are under the control of the Holy Spirit and not resort to our own sinful and fleshly tactics.

### Questions to Consider

What has primarily shaped your view of the topic of anger — Scripture or some other source?

Have you found yourself trying to justify harmful anger under the guise of it being a "righteous anger"?

What are some issues on which you perhaps should feel more righteous anger than you currently do? What should you do in response to things that should provoke righteous anger in your life?

# 3

# What Causes Anger?

*Israel:* I had quite a surprise the other day. My phone buzzed, alerting me of a new voice mail. As I listened, I was at first confused, then shocked and disappointed. The call was inadvertent. Someone had "pocket dialed" me (when the phone randomly dials someone in the phone directory).

I listened intently for the next 2 minutes and 40 seconds to a marital screaming match. This Christian couple, who I know personally, is well known in their community and respected in their church. On the outside, they are the epitome of marital bliss. But this phone call revealed an angry, vengeful, hateful, and profane side of their marriage that most others would never know.

How common is this? We had a discussion recently with a friend of ours who was raised by missionary parents. She described how her parents often conducted marriage seminars and would sit together on stage, hold hands, and gaze lovingly into each other's eyes. But it was all a façade. Behind the charade, their marriage teemed with anger, bitterness, and unforgiveness. They eventually divorced, leaving a devastating impact on their own children.

It is a shame that too often we are more concerned about what others think of us (our reputation) than we are with what God knows about us (our character).

How would our lives be different if we knew that video cameras were on in every room in our home, broadcasting all of our words and actions? The fact that we are content to live one way in public, and yet drop our guard and belittle and berate those who live closest to us, reveals hypocrisy of the worst sort. Children are very astute. They listen to what we teach them, but they observe our actions.

People can talk a good talk, but what you really believe is lived out in your actions. If our children do not experience the transformative power of the gospel lived out in the reality of our own family life, they will doubt the sincerity of our profession and the reality of the promised change offered in Scripture.

## Where Does Anger Come From?

### Self-Defense

Before anger ever becomes an emotion, it is first a physical impulse. We were divinely created with chemical reactions that fire in our brain whenever our life is threatened. This is a wonderful gift. Imagine that you are walking down the sidewalk and suddenly you see a pit bull running toward you, dragging his leash behind him. Something in his eyes (and teeth) tells you that he is not coming for a mere social visit! What happens? You are suddenly hit with a bolt of adrenaline. As this chemical impulse rages through your system, you are faced with two options: fight or flight. You will either defend, flee, or attack.

These three responses are key to understanding relationships as well. Your adrenal glands are part of the endocrine system in your body that produces adrenaline, a hormone that increases heart rate and blood flow, providing special strength for you to defend your life. After the initial physiological surge of adrenaline (medically known as epinephrine), a more rational side of our brains begin to be engaged. When you hit your thumb with a hammer, you are not choosing an emotion of anger; you are experiencing an unsolicited physical reaction. But that rush of adrenaline usually demands to be expressed in some way. If you don't run or exert physical energy in some way, you begin to look for other creative ways to release the newly found tension.

You might say something — maybe a lot of somethings — that perhaps you wish the children hadn't heard. You might throw something (the hammer is still handy). You might kick something. These are decisions that are distinct from, but very closely linked to, the initial physical impulse. But as your brain becomes more engaged in the process, your reason and decision-making processes become more acute. Very often, you begin to problem solve (even subconsciously). "Who was the stupid owner who let go of the dog's leash?" Or "Why did I hit my thumb? It couldn't have been my fault. I'm a skilled, professional adult. Whose idea was it to build these stupid shelves anyway? Oh yes . . . it was my wife's idea. Why does she always try to ruin my Saturdays with her honey-do lists when I could be doing something worthwhile?" Do you see where this is going? Suddenly, this event is connected to other events from the past that you also found undesirable, and now you are well on your way to a marital confrontation.

**Expectations**

The Book of James (4:1) tells us that anger comes from desires. Another word for this is expectations. All of us have an inherent sense of how the world should work. This is called our "world-view." It is like a set of lenses through which we interpret all of life and reality. This view of our existence is formed very early, beginning as soon as we are born. Our experiences shape our expectations. We expect that our mother will feed us, clothe us, and meet all of our needs. With each additional life experience, we gain more expectations. When our expectations are not satisfied, we feel threatened.

Very often, anger is a defense mechanism that we utilize, not only to protect our physical well-being, but also our emotional and/or spiritual well-being. One way to think of this is that we have an outside person (or physical body) and an inside person (our soul, or the real us). Either one of these can feel threatened.

Our beliefs, values, and convictions are, in many ways, an extension of us; of our inside person. When someone challenges our deeply treasured viewpoints and biases, we don't feel safe. We get defensive. People even get angry at times when others challenge their theological assumptions. Because what we believe is so intrinsically linked to our personhood, we often can't accept someone rejecting our viewpoints. It feels too much like they are rejecting us as a person.

Not only do our expectations drive the way we think life should work, but we are also uniquely created in the image of God. One of God's attributes is justice.

### Justice

When our view of how things should go is violated, we often respond in anger. This was the scenario in the first murder. Cain had a view of what should happen in his relationship with his brother. Things didn't go the way he planned, so he became angry and murdered his brother.

It is interesting to me, from my study on the topic, that anger as a force for justice may be the only biblically justifiable application of it. Beyond that, I can't find any place in Scripture that allows for anger to be used in the defense of ourselves, personally and individually, but instead, only on behalf of others (the widow, the foreigner, the oppressed, those being led away to slaughter, orphans, the poor, etc.).

Pragmatism (the belief that we can use whatever means we want as long as it brings about our desired outcome) is not a Christian philosophy. We do not have the luxury of implementing any old method to accomplish our goals. In our anger (at the injustice we see in the world around us), we do not have the option to sin in our response.

Regarding our own personal irritations, we have a moral command to not administer punishment on those who have hurt us. The Bible tells us that vengeance (getting even and ensuring that the other person gets what they have coming to them) belongs to God alone. He will repay. We must not. This is not to say that we do not use proper legal means (court systems, the police, etc.) to ensure that those who have done us harm are appropriately brought to justice, but it does mean that our motivation must be redemptive, for the good of society, and even for the perpetrator of the crime; that he or she will have an opportunity in the process to recognize his or her offense or evil and seek repentance. We can be rightfully angry at the evil of the person's crime, or the hideousness of his or her sin, but we must seek his or her ultimate repentance and reconciliation to God.

### Getting to the Root

While the impulse of self-protection, caused by the physical reaction occurring in our brains when we feel threatened, is certainly not sin, what we choose to do with that impulse often is. When we lash out at others, wrongly blame them, or allow bitterness to take hold in our hearts, we have crossed the line from a physical reaction to making a moral (or immoral, in this case) choice.

It is our firm belief that it is almost impossible to sin, in any capacity, without the following three conditions being present: self-love, pride, and unbelief. Let's explore how these root issues relate to anger.

### Self-Love

We were created to love, just as we were created to worship. In fact, it is impossible for us not to love, or to worship. The question is, what are we loving? In 1 Corinthians 13:2, the Apostle Paul asks rhetorically, "What am I if I don't have love?" But in one sense, when we are failing to love others it is because we are enraptured in ourselves. Jesus commanded us to "love your neighbor as yourself" (Mark 12:31; Matt. 22:39). There is a clear presupposition here that we are already loving ourselves, and now we need to extend that care and concern that we show to our own well-being to those around us. We are told in Scripture, "No one ever hated his own flesh, but nourishes and cherishes it . . ." (Eph. 5:28–30).

What is ironic is that even what we call self-loathing, or self-harming, or low self-esteem is still, very much, an obsessive compulsive focus on ourselves. C.S. Lewis wrote that true humility isn't thinking less of ourselves; it is thinking of ourselves less.[1]

Quite often, we are the center of our own little universe. This often negatively impacts our relationships with others. When our sense of justice is violated, we come unglued. When the perfect little world we created in our minds isn't panning out the way we hoped, we lash out (to defend ourselves and our ideals). One author expressed it this way:

> How does anger help? It is actually pretty easy: we feel the most anger when the idols at the center of our lives are threatened. Why? Because idols need defending. False gods are not capable of bringing us real joy, providing peace of mind, carrying our hopes and dreams, or meeting our basic spiritual needs. Therefore, real life constantly exposes their inadequacies, and so we become threatened and angry on their behalf.[2]

## Pride

Very closely connected to self-love is pride. Pride can take on many different forms, and just like anger, it exists on a spectrum, or a continuum. We can easily scroll through the menu options from self-confidence, to haughtiness, to condescension of others, to arrogance, to megalomania, narcissism, and delusions of grandeur.

Pride is the belief that my needs, my wants, my desires, my expectations, my hopes, my feelings, my comfort, and my protection must be achieved and maintained above all else. Nothing and no one had better come between me and my desired life. When my mirror pool of the perfect life is shattered by a pebble of irritation or annoyance, or a rock of wrongdoing, someone is going to pay.

---

1. My summary of C.S. Lewis's teaching in *Mere Christianity* (New York, NY: Harper Collins Edition, 2001), p. 121–128.
2. Andrew D. Lester, *Anger: Discovering your Spiritual Ally* (Louisville, KY: Westminster John Knox Press, 2007), p. 110.

Pride is very closely linked to our own self-image and self-worth. Our sense of worth is very closely tied to our values and ideals. There are things that we believe and cherish, and when those things are threatened, we panic. For example, a mother may have a value or an expectation (a "desire" as James calls it) of having a clean house. When her four-year-old daily trashes that value or desire, her emotional self (not her physical self this time) is threatened. She may have a value of looking nice and being attractive to her husband. If he destroys that hope with unkind words about her physique, her emotional self is threatened. She may have a value of her children being kind and respectful to others and, therefore, being admired by friends and neighbors (since she sees her children as a reflection of herself and her parenting). When her 15-year-old tells an inappropriate joke at a relative's wedding and everyone feels awkward and uncomfortable, she is hurt emotionally. Again, just as with the pit bull, she is put in a fight or flight pattern. The impulse of anger is not a sin here. She is feeling the need to defend her (emotional) life and has just been supplied with the adrenaline to do so. But it is at this moment, if she isn't careful, that pride will exert itself and she will act in her best interests rather than the best interests of the other person. She may respond in self-love and self-protection rather than true love for the offending party.

Now let us be clear here. The four-year-old needs to be trained. The husband needs to be lovingly informed about how his words are making his bride feel. The mouthy teenager needs to learn respect and propriety. We're not advocating being a doormat for others to wipe their muddy boots on. Far from it! But why should you act in the appropriate way? Why should you speak? Why should you (lovingly) confront? It needs to be for the good of the other person. That is what love looks like. Defending yourself and your rights for your own sake is not what Jesus called us to do. When we defend our justifiable, God-given rights, we do so from a posture of love for others, knowing that standing up for what is right is best for the perpetrator, the whole of society, and, lastly, ourselves. We love our neighbors (or family members) in the same way we want them to love us (in a redemptive way that considers our ultimate best interests).

## Unbelief

We have never heard anyone link anger to the sin of unbelief before, but we think there is a connection. Constantly in Scripture, we are reminded about the importance of faith. "Without faith, it is impossible to please [God]" (Heb. 11:6). "Whatever does not proceed from faith is sin" (Rom. 14:23). We can't even be saved without faith: "For by grace you have been saved through faith" (Eph. 2:8). If you don't have faith, you don't belong to God. The opposite of faith is doubt, or unbelief.

Because the word "faith" is used so frequently in Christian circles, and means a lot of things to a lot of people, I'd like to substitute a different word that might help you understand the concept better: trust. Do you trust God? Trusting God necessitates an understanding of His sovereignty. You have to know and believe that God is infinitely all-powerful, all-knowing, and all-loving. If you lose belief in any one of these vital doctrines, you are no longer worshiping and believing in God, because those are several of God's essential, irreducible attributes.

This protective reaction we have — that we must defend our lives (physical, emotional, financial, and spiritual) — comes from a lack of trust in God. Essentially, even though we are not thinking about it cognitively, we are refusing to believe in God's moral goodness. We are doubting that He truly loves us and has our best interests in mind. We are appalled by the disruption that He has allowed into our little idealistic world, and we are afraid. Fear is *always* linked to unbelief. When you are afraid, you have doubt rather than trust. (Israel explains this in a chapter entitled, "Why Are You Afraid?" in his book *Questions Jesus Asks*.)[3]

---

3. Israel Wayne, *Questions Jesus Asks* (Green Forest, AR: New Leaf Press, 2015).

Again, this is not the instinctive physical reaction of fear that you experience when a pit bull is charging at you, but the emotion that springs forth later after the physical impulse. The ongoing, abiding foreboding that something bad is going to happen to you (or to those you love) is *not* from God but from the evil one. "For God gave us a spirit not of fear but of power and love and self-control" (2 Tim. 1:7).

When we feel attacked or hurt in some way, we often lash out and defend ourselves because we feel that no one else will. In a moment of pain and doubt, it certainly doesn't seem that God is going to take care of us. He isn't going to rescue us from this cancer, or that stain on the carpet, or those unkind words from a coworker, or this credit card bill that we can't afford to pay, or the car that just damaged our fender. God is obviously not interested in protecting us and looking out for us to the level that we think He should, and so we feel we have to swing into action and save ourselves.

Anger is often our attempt to right the wrongs and injustices done to us, or those we love, and bring our idealistic world back into alignment. In that moment, it is very possible to cross the appropriate line of responsibility and self-initiative, to becoming something we were never meant to be: God. We are not the judge of the universe. We are not the one who has to mete out justice and ensure that those who have hurt or offended us get what they have coming to them. It's not our place. Our place is to let go and let God. Our role is to love, to forgive, to seek to restore and reconcile. That's our mandate.

This is where we need to go back to 1 Corinthians 13 and apply faith, hope, and love. Believe that God has everything under control. Put your hope and confidence in Him. Rest in the fact that He loves you infinitely, and nothing will touch your life that has not been filtered through the hands of your loving Father.

## The Law of First Mention

In Biblical hermeneutics (how to study the Bible and understand it in its context), there is a view that you can often understand a concept most accurately by looking at the first place it is mentioned in Scripture. This place of first mention is often one of the most simple and basic explanations of the idea and helps to shed light on subsequent uses of the word or doctrine.

In the first relational conflict on the planet, we see anger. This sets the tone for and helps us to understand some of the root concepts behind relational conflict for the millennia to come.

> Now Adam knew Eve his wife, and she conceived and bore Cain, saying, "I have gotten a man with the help of the LORD." And again, she bore his brother Abel. Now Abel was a keeper of sheep, and Cain a worker of the ground. In the course of time Cain brought to the LORD an offering of the fruit of the ground, and Abel also brought of the firstborn of his flock and of their fat portions. And the LORD had regard for Abel and his offering, but for Cain and his offering he had no regard. So Cain was very angry, and his face fell. The LORD said to Cain, "Why are you angry, and why has your face fallen? If you do well, will you not be accepted? And if you do not do well, sin is crouching at the door. Its desire is for you, but you must rule over it" (Gen. 4:1–7).

### Envy

Inherent in Cain's despising of Abel is envy. His brother is accepted by God, and he is not.

> But if you have bitter jealousy and selfish ambition in your hearts, do not boast and be false to the truth. This is not the wisdom that comes down from above, but is earthly, unspiritual, demonic. For where jealousy and selfish ambition exist, there will be disorder

and every vile practice. But the wisdom from above is first pure, then peaceable, gentle, open to reason, full of mercy and good fruits, impartial and sincere. And a harvest of righteousness is sown in peace by those who make peace (James 3:14–18).

Envy or jealousy is ultimately rooted in dissatisfaction with God. It is an implicit accusation against God's justice. It suggests that God has not been fair in His dealings with us. Harboring an accusation against God is a grave and dangerous sin of presumption.

## Rebellion

We see in Cain's reaction the triumvirate of evil: pride, self-love, and unbelief. Together, these always result in another "irreducibly complex" element of sin: rebellion. We want to define the terms of our life. We want to decide for ourselves what is right and wrong. We want to take matters into our own hands, and ensure that justice (as we have defined it) is served the way we think it should be. It's a kind of self-expressed idolatry. We are trying to be our own little God. But God will have no other gods before Him. He alone is God, and our job is to submit to His Lordship.

Submitting our "right" to anger to Christ's rule and reign is one of our chief goals in the continuing process of Christian sanctification.

### Roadmap to Freedom

If you find yourself in a habit of responding in anger to others, here are the initial steps to break free:

1. Evaluate where you are on the anger spectrum.
2. Recognize your need to change, and your inability to do it on your own.
3. Ask God to forgive you and change your heart.
4. Believe that God can and will change you.
5. Saturate your mind in God's Word, memorize it, and apply it.

6. Recognize your anger triggers.
7. Confess and repent *every time* you blow it.
8. Strategically practice speaking words of encouragement to others. It will help to rewire your brain with thoughts of gratitude rather than bitterness and anger.
9. It generally takes 30 days to create a new habit. Disrupt your old patterns, and intentionally replace them with new ones.
10. Be willing to seek accountability and prayer support from others.
11. Journal your progress (and setbacks). This will give you perspective over time.
12. Tenaciously guard your daily time alone with Jesus, and don't neglect your spiritual disciplines.

Remember that walking in the Spirit is the way that you will stop fulfilling the lusts of the flesh (see Gal. 5:16). It is God who will change you as you remain in Him.

The Holy Spirit can and does change our hearts, actions, and words. Participate with Him in His work!

# 4

# Provoking Our Children to Wrath

*Israel:* Someone recently asked me, "What makes you uniquely qualified to address this issue of anger?" The unspoken insinuation was that I probably don't know much about this topic because I'm a low-key, easygoing guy. The fact that I am known for that is nothing but a tribute to the grace and mercy of God.

My life, growing up, was very complex. My parents divorced when I was six years old. My mother remarried a man who was very physically, emotionally, verbally, and psychologically abusive. Despite the craziness of our situation, my mother did her best to provide sacrificially for us and to raise us as best she could. She was very limited by the chaos of the environment in which we lived, but despite being a recipient of abuse herself, she did all she could to care for us.

My stepfather was not just a guy who occasionally flew off the handle and got angry. In my opinion, he was cruel and sadistic. He seemed to premeditate ways to make situations turn out really awful. We lived in constant fear, always walking on eggshells and trying not to interact with him any more than absolutely necessary.

The two factors that influence a child more than any other are:

1. *Time.* Whoever spends the most time with a child has the greatest ability to shape and mold his or her beliefs and behavior.
2. *Affirmation.* Everyone innately craves acceptance. We all want to be loved and liked. Even if a parent spends time with his or her child, yet neglects to show proper love and affection, the child will eventually seek to meet those needs elsewhere.

In case you have ever wondered if anger is a learned behavior, the Scripture makes it clear that, to a great extent, it is. There is little doubt that anger is an innate part of our fleshly nature, so we will all deal with it to some degree, but it can also be inculcated as a besetting sin through constant demonstration and example.

> Make no friendship with a man given to anger, nor go with a wrathful man, lest you learn his ways and entangle yourself in a snare (Prov. 22:24–25).

I so realize the truth of this verse. It is a very interesting phenomenon, but I have learned that if you cannot forgive those who have hurt you, you often become what you hate. How many times have you known someone who sees the wrong that has been done to them, they despise it in their abuser, but they perpetuate those same negative traits and pass them on in toxic relationships with others?

I remember when I was 12, just after having been severely physically attacked by my stepfather, he stared me down (as he awaited the arrival of the police who were going to arrest him). He looked into my eyes and said, "I hate you. If I go to prison, it may seem like a long time to you, but it won't to me. I'll eventually get out. I'll find you. I'll hunt you down, and I'll kill you." (Not that he hadn't tried to do just that only moments before.)

Although I had never felt this before in my life, I looked him in the eyes and told him, "I hate you too!" And I meant it. Unfortunately, he was released on a one-year probation.

Sometime after that year (he was careful to never violate his probation), he was put out of the house once again by the police. Not long after that, my mother had to leave to go to the store. She told me, "Whatever you do, don't open the door if he comes back." Not to worry.

I didn't need to be told that. I knew what would happen if he came back.

Come back he did. When we did not open the door, he tried to break it down. Little did he know that I was sitting just behind that door with a loaded 12-gauge shotgun (which he had often used to threaten us). My little sisters were with me, and there was no way I was going to allow them to be harmed. For some reason (which I now understand was the providence of God), the wimpy latch held, and he couldn't force entry (even though he was a big man). If he had, he would have met his end, and I would have had to live with that scenario for the rest of my life.

It's so amazing to think back on one's life and consider how differently everything could have played out. It wouldn't have taken very much for my life to take a completely different turn. Even in the midst of all of the pain and the confusion of our lives, God was there. He was at work, slowly and subtly leading and guiding us.

### Becoming What You Hate

I lived in this dysfunctional lifestyle for nine long and excruciating years. When a young man experiences that kind of physical abuse for the most formative years of his upbringing, it has a tremendously damaging effect. It wrecks your sense of manhood and masculinity. It strips you of any sense of what normal family life is supposed to look like. And perhaps most damaging, it teaches you, erroneously, how to respond to pressure and stress. You lash out.

I was always a little shrimpy kid. I once went to an amusement park with my friends and was the only kid my age who couldn't ride the rides because I didn't weigh enough. I joined the church Bible quizzing team and didn't weigh enough to make the seat buzzer go off! (I wasn't malnourished; it was just my metabolism at the time.) But when bullies would try to pick on me, I'd take them out, even when they were much bigger than me. The reason was, they were just looking for some fun. They had size, but I had rage.

All of those years of abuse had made me very volatile. I was explosive, like a walking bomb. You had better not set me off. I began to scare even myself. I soon realized that I wasn't really in control of my temper. Instead, it had control of me.

### A Change

When I was 12, my mother, who had always sent us to church and tried to raise us to be Christians, met God in a very radical way. Her surrender to Christ was an essential part in our eventually being able to break free from the horror of our life and start a new one. We left our state and fled my stepfather. We dropped out of existence for a couple of years, and were discipled in a church over a thousand miles away. It was a clean start. Those people loved us and taught us, from Scripture and example, what it meant to be a godly family.

I remember one day, at the age of 15, sitting in the middle of a church service. There were hundreds of other people around me listening to the message. I wasn't listening. I was having my own private conversation with God. I remember asking God, "Why is it that You don't love me? I totally believe that You are who You say You are. You are the Creator. Jesus, I believe You are God in the flesh. I've always believed all of the essential doctrines of the faith from as far back as I can remember. I believe the Bible from cover to cover. I believe that You are omnipotent, omniscient, and omnipresent. I believe You can do anything You want to. But what I'm wondering right now is why You don't care. Why have You allowed the things that You have allowed in my life? I'm not struggling with the all-knowing aspect of Your character, but I'm questioning the all-loving part. Is this just some kind of cruel and sadistic joke to You? Does all of this mean nothing to You?"

I was hurting. I didn't need more theology at that moment. I needed love. Now I'm not an experiential sort of guy. You don't base your salvation on emotions and feelings. You base your faith on the death, burial, and Resurrection of the only true and living Son of God. But experiences are not always bad. Sometimes God allows us to have experiences just to demonstrate Himself to us in a real and genuine way. We are, after all, emotional people as well as cerebral ones. God understands this, and He sometimes speaks to our hearts, as well as to our minds.

In that moment, I felt bathed in the love of God. I felt, in a very tangible way, not only the nearness of His presence but the infilling of His kindness. I felt Him reassure me that everything I had been through was known by Him and was not without meaning or purpose. As with Job, I didn't get all of the answers to my questions, but I was granted the gift of His touch and His favor. I needed to feel the truth of His love, and not merely believe it. Again, it is our faith in Christ that saves us, not our feelings, but there is also nothing wrong with proper feelings that accompany our faith (trust).

Not many weeks after that, I remember praying about my future. I prayed a very intense prayer, which I meant with all of my heart. I said, "Lord, at some point in my life, do You plan for me to marry and have a family? Because if You do, I'm afraid of what I might do to them. I've read all of the statistics that indicate that I will simply be a repeat of my stepfather. I know that the likelihood is that I will perpetuate the cycle of violence. I couldn't bear to do that. If I would ever look into my wife's eyes, or my children's eyes, and see fear, because of me . . . then please just kill me now! I'd rather die than do to another person what has been done to me."

That is how serious I was about this issue. I knew that anger had so gripped my life that I had no viable way of managing it. There was no way that I was going to just be able to "count to ten" or utilize some kind of "mind over matter" approach. I was in too deep. I was utterly helpless.

God met me at the point of my need, and He just supernaturally took away the rage! Of course, I had to participate in the miracle. Just like the crippled man who had to stand up or the blind man who had to open his eyes, I had a part to play as well. I had to be willing to exchange my right to be bitter and angry in exchange for God's love and mercy. It was an amazing and extraordinary trade!

Now God doesn't deal with any two people the same way. God doesn't simply heal everyone in the same way He did with me. And even in my own life, while I have never again had the same kinds of extreme feelings of anger that possessed me for so long, I have had to learn principles of how to walk in victory over the less extreme spectrum issues associated with anger. I get annoyed, frustrated, stressed out, irritated, and even mildly angry, just like most other people. So regardless of where you are on the spectrum, or how much battle lies ahead for you in this area, a slow healing is just as miraculous as a quick one.

### How We Provoke Our Children to Wrath

> Fathers, do not provoke your children to anger, but
> bring them up in the discipline and instruction of the
> Lord (Eph. 6:4).

This verse is proof-positive that anger is not merely something we can take out on our children, but it is also something that we can (even inadvertently) cultivate in them. One of the most harmful effects of anger is what it does to the inside world of a child.

Some researchers do studies on various approaches to discipline and how they are received by children. Do certain approaches cultivate resentment or violent behavior in children? The one factor that almost never gets included in such studies is perhaps the most important component: anger. Regardless of which approach you use for disciplining your children (even if you implement a completely hands-free approach), if you are correcting your children in anger, you are doing it wrong.

In his book, *Full-Time Parenting: A Guide to Family-Based Discipleship*,[1] Israel explains in much more detail what a biblical approach to child discipline should look like. That is not the focus of this book. However, you should be mindful that it is not appropriate to take out your frustrations on your child. All discipline needs to be redemptive, for the good of the child.

### Are You a Thermometer or a Thermostat?

As a parent, it is really common to see things in your children that you don't like. At times, their behavior baffles the mind. *Where* do they learn these things? You see them fighting among themselves, being selfish, yelling at their siblings, hurting others, breaking things, etc. It is clear that the emotional and spiritual temperature of the home is not what you want it to be.

Spending time with your children is like looking at a thermometer. You need to intentionally consider from time to time

---

1. Israel Wayne, *Full-Time Parenting: A Guide to Family-Based Discipleship* (Covert, MI: Wisdom's Gate, 2012).

how your children are progressing in terms of their love for others, and their willingness and/or ability to get along with and serve their siblings and friends.

When things are not looking good is the time to ask yourself: "What do I need to change about myself?" The fact is, as parents we are the thermostats for our family. Men are often the thermostats for their wives, and both parents set the emotional temperature for their children.

Oftentimes, men bring their stresses and frustration from work home and offload their pent-up annoyances on their wives. The wives often internalize this and then externalize it in angry outbursts to the children. The children then act out in negative ways and, in turn, annoy their parents with their bad behavior. Who will break this cycle?

You can rest assured it will not be the children who take the high road and make the necessary changes. It will have to be you.

If you don't like what you see in your little ones, then you need make changes in yourself. You can't create a peaceful and calm attitude in your children through instruction alone. However, you can create it by demonstrating it through your actions.

### How Can You Help Your Children Overcome Their Anger?

When we respond poorly to our stresses and frustrations, we create patterns for our children to follow. Sometimes, because we were provoked to wrath, we inadvertently provoke our children to wrath as well. What a vicious cycle!

So how do we help our children to overcome their anger? Well, the first thing is that we teach them God's standard, and we explain to them that nobody gets a free pass on being obedient to God. Not them, and not us. There may be a sense in which, as a parent, you are afraid to deal with the sin in their life, because you see the log in your own eye (so to speak). So what does Jesus tell us to do? Deal with the log in our own eye, so we can deal with the log in our child's eye (Matt. 7:3–5). Let them know that we are all together in this process of sanctification.

Teach them how to use words of kindness to turn away anger. "A soft answer turns away wrath, but a harsh word stirs up anger" (Prov. 15:1).

Teach them how to think of others as more important than themselves. "Do nothing from selfish ambition or conceit, but in humility count others more significant than yourselves" (Phil. 2:3).

Teach them to be quick to forgive their siblings and others when they are offended. "Be kind to one another, tenderhearted, forgiving one another, as God in Christ forgave you" (Eph. 4:32).

"Bearing with one another and, if one has a complaint against another, forgiving each other; as the Lord has forgiven you, so you also must forgive" (Col. 3:13).

Teach them to take complete ownership of their faults when they sin against another person through their anger. "I confess my iniquity; I am sorry for my sin" (Ps. 38:18).

"Therefore, confess your sins to one another and pray for one another, that you may be healed" (James 5:16).

Teach them how to use words to encourage and build up their siblings and friends. Teach them to use their tongues to build up, and not to tear down. "Let no corrupting talk come out of your mouths, but only such as is good for building up, as fits the occasion, that it may give grace to those who hear" (Eph. 4:29).

### Breaking the Tattling Syndrome

One of the ways children express anger created by their siblings is through tattling. Ironically, when we have talked with many parents, this is one of the primary childhood behaviors that they say makes *them* angry as parents! So what is a good way to deal with this frustrating scenario?

Early on in our parenting journey, we realized we needed some kind of system for our children to follow when one child offended another (either personally, or by not following house rules). Thus, out of desperation, we began pondering how to go about setting up a system. Finally, it occurred to us that the principles laid out in Matthew 18 fit pretty closely with what we needed! Our children are the future Church, so it only made sense to help set their feet to walk in this pattern early on.

This is what I taught my youngsters to do when a sibling acted wrongly:

1. *Gently* speak to your brother or sister and ask him or her to stop. Remind the sibling of what is right. As much as possible, I encourage my children to remind each other of what "Mama and Papa have *said*" — thus hearkening to parental authority, and not a sibling's whim. This is what we do for each other as brothers and sisters in Christ, right? Sharing the Word of the Lord with one another as adults takes the discussion out of the realm of opinion or "he said, she said" and back to the powerful Word.

2. If that brother or sister will not respond, send them (and go with them) to Mom and Dad so that the offender can tell on himself. This is where we've sought to bring tattling to an end. Each child is required to tell on themselves about their own wrongdoing. Naturally, we sometimes end up with an overzealous child who wishes to get others into trouble ("He was whistling! I told him to stop and he wouldn't!"), and that requires a different approach. Overall, a child telling on himself helps us as parents get to the heart of the matter much more quickly. The accountability of the first child's report is also helpful in deciphering what happened.

3. If the brother or sister still refuses to listen, or to go with you to his or her parents when requested, you may come and tell Mom and Dad. This helps us as parents not to have major things slip by unnoticed.

We do need to know what is going on, and at this point, a child has done his duty by encouraging his deviant sibling to act rightly. Always, always, we encourage our children to bring any kind of reprimand to their sibling's attention in a kind, loving way. The natural tendency for children is to become angry and proud and seek to deal with the situation on their own. They need to be reminded that it is not their place to discipline their sibling. That's Mom and Dad's job. Theirs is to walk through the scenario lovingly.

Many times a family will have a "fixer" — the child who *loves* to "remind" his brothers or sisters about Mom and Dad's words. They often don't know how to handle their own emotions in difficult situations. This child often has a very strong sense of justice and wants to be God's agent to dish it out. When they can't walk through a disagreement without being annoyed and angry, they need to back off.

For example, we have two boys who share a room. One is a tidy, and one is a messy. The tidy has all of his clothes match, every hair in place, and his space arranged in an orderly manner. The other is a walking cyclone of chaos. This provides lots of opportunity for anger on both sides. The older one, who is tidy, will verbally grind down on the younger messy, who is not only annoying with his own lack of cleanliness, but invades his brother's turf as well.

We try to explain to both boys that God has placed them together for them to learn how to walk in love toward each other. If you can learn to love your difficult sibling, you can learn to love just about anyone!

> If anyone says, "I love God," and hates his brother, he is a liar; for he who does not love his brother whom he has seen cannot love God whom he has not seen (1 John 4:20).

### Parenting Is Discipleship

Jesus said, "A disciple is not above his teacher, but everyone when he is fully trained will be like his teacher" (Luke 6:40).

We teach our children through two primary means:

1. Systematic instruction in the truth
2. Daily personal example and demonstration

We need to provide our children with a proper theology of relationships, but we also need to seek to faithfully walk out what we want to see in them. Far more is caught than taught in parenting. Your children hear your words, but they embrace far more from your actions.

### Questions to Consider

In what ways has your childhood contributed to the way you deal with stress and irritation? Consider the same about your spouse. Do you handle aggravation similarly or differently?

Can you see ways in which you contribute to your child's anger?

Do you see your children expressing anger toward you or their siblings?

What are some guidelines you'd like to help establish in your home to promote peace among your children?

# 5

# Trigger Happy —
# What Sets You Off?

There are some stresses and circumstances we can't escape. However, sometimes there are "anger triggers" we allow into our lives. Slowing down in a quiet moment to make a purposeful list of personal anger triggers can help us evaluate and, as able, remove those triggers.

### Recognizing and Dealing with Your Anger Triggers

Not all parenting stress is created equal. For instance, walking into your sister's wedding two minutes late and finding out your baby just had a diaper explosion all over your lovely outfit is one level of stress. Learning your ten-year-old has started a fire in his closet with his new electronics set (that he wasn't supposed to use without permission!) is quite another.

The first example is in no way the baby's fault. We may feel anger toward her for causing us trouble, but it isn't reasonable. On the other hand, we expect older children to "know better." So when we become angry in such a situation, we tend to feel totally justified. Yet, even when direct disregard is given to Mom and Dad's words, do we truly have a right to be angry?

Our children will provide a plethora of opportunities for us as parents to learn self-control. From a parent's view, they seem to purposely do things that infuriate us and drive us over the edge. Other times, however, our parental anger actually has next to nothing to do with our children. Maybe we even recognize that truth in the heat of the moment. They didn't necessarily *do* anything all that bad; we just *feel* upset, angered, and irritable. So if the problem lies with us, what are we doing wrong that sets us up for failure? Let's look at some common anger triggers together. Maybe you'll identify with one or two of your own.

> *Brook:* **Lotsa Latte?** Let's start with caffeine. Now don't get me wrong. I have really come to enjoy a cup of coffee. After our seventh child was born, I was living in the drowsy, sleepless-nights-newborn stage. My dad, a life-long coffee drinker, gave me a cup of coffee and, wow, it

was like the lights went on! I could think again! I became a fan, and just a little bit of coffee now and then helped keep me alert when I needed to be awake. So if a cup is good, well, how much better is two cups? However, I noticed there is a fine line for me, somewhere around two and three cups, that the coffee goes beyond just giving me a little energy to actually causing me to feel antsy, irritable, and quick-tempered. Ever been there?

Once I could identify the cause of my touchy feelings, I realized I needed to have some serious coffee restrictions. The helpful boost of adrenaline simply wasn't worth it to me, or my family, to introduce something that would make me prone to anger. Definitely a "disposable stress" I could do without! I'd like to briefly add that sugar, or underlying food sensitivities/allergies, can also have the same effect by raising our physical stress levels. While we are always responsible for our attitudes, why in the world would we feed ourselves something that makes the battle against stress and anger more difficult?

**Clutter and Chaos:** Numerous studies have shown that a cluttered home does indeed wear on the nerves of its residents. How could it not? When something goes missing among the clutter, it can take hours to relocate! That alone is a stress all of us could do without. The cumulative effect of living in clutter and chaos (who knows when the next meal will be, or who is supposed to be doing what and when) is a continual low-grade stress situation that makes it all the easier to jump to anger when something (inevitably) goes wrong. While it may not be a total cure, creating a habit of decluttering and scheduling can go a long way toward kicking this stress to the curb.

Two years ago, I finally gained the bravery to stop endlessly "organizing" and start decluttering. While we still have a long way to go before we reach any kind of minimalist lifestyle, the progress we have made in simplifying our practical life has made the functioning of our family much easier. Clutter, and too much undirected time, is stressful for everyone in the family. Who needs that kind of stress?

**Perfectionism:** At some point, perfectionistic or not, all parents will face the stress of unmet expectations. This can be tricky ground. There is no "one size fits all" answer, because there are so many variables involved (age of child, training given for specific job given, etc.). In short, parents run into not only a child's ability to perform his or her given task, but also the child's moral character to live by what he or she knows is right. This kind of stress is harder to "put away," because it pops up in our lives so unexpectedly.

Honestly evaluating (husbands and wives together!) the degree of your own perfectionistic leanings is a needful start. If your family is afraid to move around in your house for fear of setting you off, you can be pretty sure there is a problem. On the other hand, you do want to teach your children to strive for excellence in all they do, so balance is needed.

Having realistic expectations is key. You must determine if your child is too young to accomplish what you are expecting or if you haven't trained him or her properly. Many times when we are frustrated with our children it is because we have *told* them to do something, but we haven't *shown* them *how* to do what is required of them. So they do a sloppy, half-baked job, and we get angry. Whose fault is this really? This is where the mirror shines brightly back at us as parents.

Stress, while it may have been your go-to in the past, Perfectionistic Mom or Dad, won't help you or your child meet your long-term goals. Step back from the situation and ask, "Am I willing to take the time to lovingly walk my child through how to do this job correctly?" Replacing the leaning toward stress with seizing the opportunity to train your children will go a long way toward reducing anger triggers in your home.

**Late for Appointments:** I've been looking for years for the button on children that turns them on "focused to get ready to leave" . . . without success. We're not fooling our families by hollering and stressing on a Sunday morning at home, then acting "spiritual" at service. Hypocrisy and anger obviously need to be weeded out of our lives at every point, but do yourself a favor and manage your time well so that you can kindly lead your children in managing their time well. Yes, even on any old Sunday morning. Practical tips like laying out shoes and clothing, belts, Bibles, and coats the night before are lifesavers for us. Other simple ideas, like serving a "make-ahead" breakfast or waking up a little earlier, can also serve to reduce that "Sunday morning rush." It is no mere accident that the biblical Sabbath began on Friday night and people took that Friday to prepare for the day of rest. We could learn from this principle.

**Interruptions:** Little children, by and large, know nothing other than interrupting. Nothing. Baby has always been first in Mommy and Daddy's life, and they've been able to ask for whatever they needed whenever they wanted. Never mind the fact that baby is now getting on to 2, 3, 4, and then 11 years of age! That little one will only and ever interrupt until taught otherwise.

So why does it anger us as parents when these little people obliviously prance up to us, while we are in the middle of an important phone call, to ask if they can have a popsicle? Or jump on our lap while we are visiting with a friend and ask to go to the park (or more embarrassingly, go home)? This is again one of those anger triggers that we'd like to do without, but it will take some self-control on our part, and some training of our youngsters.

The root of this issue is control. We don't want to be bothered with having to deal, once again, with a halt in our plans. In our own sense of self-importance, we want to make sure the world turns on our schedule. We want to make sure that what we have planned doesn't get disrupted. I'm not saying we therefore turn our worlds to revolve around our children so that they can interrupt at any point. I am saying that we need to realize that gently teaching our children to wait when appropriate needs to get bumped up on *our* priority list. Mishandling childish interruptions through means of domination and intimidation will cause relational wounds that can be hard to mend.

The solution isn't just to visit and make phone calls when Junior is napping. Even toddlers can catch on to the idea of observing to see if Mom or Dad are busy before saying whatever is on their mind. Teaching the youngster to place his hand on the parent's arm, and waiting to be acknowledged by the parent before speaking, has worked well for us. It makes for a lot less stress and fewer socially awkward moments for both parents and children. If it is simply not a good time to reasonably interact with your child, an embracing phrase such as, "I want to hear what you have to say, but this is not a good time. Can you try to remember what you wanted to say and tell me later?" can go a long way toward connecting with your child's heart.

**Internet and Social Media:** Electronic communication can be both a blessing and a curse. We are totally for staying connected with our families and friends. Social media just takes this to a new level. Years ago we had relationships, of course, but we didn't scroll through posts from 20–50 friends in a matter of minutes. Instead, we heard or spoke with them one-on-one. Today's use of social media can leave many feeling overwhelmed as they take on the stresses and strains their friends are going through. We need to carefully watch our time online. We want to pray and encourage those we can through social media, but when we leave the social media world, we need to have something left to give to our family in the here and now. Stress we accumulate looking over everyone else's drama doesn't benefit anyone.

### Negative and Violent Media

Aggressive music and violent movies and video games can all give us surges of adrenaline, which can in turn be externalized in aggressive behavior. This is true for both us and our children. Sometimes a wise way to reduce the stress in the home is to play worshipful and melodic music quietly in the background. We should seek to make Philippians 4:8 our standard for the music and entertainment we consume.

> Finally, brothers, whatever is true, whatever is honorable, whatever is just, whatever is pure, whatever is lovely, whatever is commendable, if there is any excellence, if there is anything worthy of praise, think about these things.

*Brook:* **Negative Self-Talk (NST):** NST is speaking to oneself in overly critical, harsh, and belittling ways. Okay, I know this doesn't seem to have a lot to do with anger, or triggering anger toward our children. However, the truth is that if we engage in NST, that harsh negativity will eventually come out to bite those nearest and dearest to us. Here's why. When we speak to ourselves in harsh language, chewing ourselves out for mistakes and failures, we have thoroughly prepped and practiced just how to respond when those around us fail. Those utilizing NST live on the sharp edge of stress, and even though it is often meant to stay inside of one's head, the reality is that what we hold in our minds and hearts will come out and deeply affect others. NST is a fruit, not a root. One root is a critical, negative attitude, cultivated from a lack of a proper sense of self-worth. Often, when others have talked down to us, we embrace a negative view of ourselves and others. Another root is a perfectionistic attitude where we are hard on ourselves (and everyone else) because everything has to be just right, or we aren't happy.

I have personal experience with NST, but from a different angle. I was blessed that, growing up, my parents were pretty affirming. However, as a 13-year-old, I resorted to being very critical of myself. I desired to do well in every sphere of my life: studies, music, sewing — everything I put my hand to. But my intentions weren't all good. Partly, I wanted to shield myself from correction. I wanted to make sure I didn't allow any personal imperfection! As a young person, this mentality seemed to work pretty well for me. If I didn't achieve the perfection I wanted, my thoughts could berate myself "so that I would do better next time." However, when the clock was advanced several years down the road, and I had young children who, in the clumsy, childlike ways of youth, didn't always sweep in the corners, or scrub the grout with toothpicks like their mother, this negative self-talk spilled over onto my children. They didn't deserve it. I hadn't planned on being "that" kind of mother, but I had practiced belittling myself for so long that it had become second nature.

James 1:26 summarizes pretty well what I was doing: "If anyone thinks he is religious and does not bridle his tongue but deceives his heart, this person's religion is worthless." I thought I was so "religious" to keep myself "humble" with my nasty inside remarks to myself. It wasn't true humility at all, but rather an obsession with finding perfection. It was a pride that aimed for being above any kind of correction.

I wish I had taken heed of this verse sooner, especially resting in the second half: "Every way of a man is right in his own eyes, but the LORD weighs the heart" (Prov. 21:2). I thought my patterns were good and useful, but self-examination is only useful if we look to the Lord to help us sort through the mess.

Now a clear distinction is needed here. Please note the words I'm using: berate, belittle, harsh, criticize, etc. There are times (if we're going to walk in the light as He is in the light) that we are going to have to tell ourselves, and our children, negative things: "I was wrong" or "you were wrong, and here is what the Scripture says about. . . ." I'm not promoting a skewed self-esteem approach where we untruthfully say wrongdoing is good. There is a time for all things, including rebuking sin in our own lives and the lives of our children. There is a time for correcting and challenging, but it all must be served up on a platter of love, smothered in love, and delivered with love. Going on and on about your own or a child's wrong-doing with over-the-top critical and unkind language won't help the matter. In fact, you may just pave the way for your child to become that which you are seeking to steer him against!

When I realized that the "self-talk" I had indulged in was harming my family, I knew I needed to change. Change didn't necessarily come easily or quickly, but I knew I couldn't let the harmful patterns I had allowed in my life and home continue. While I didn't readily see that my habits were damaging me personally, I was willing to put a stop to it for the sake of my children.

I realize this topic won't apply to everyone reading this chapter, but I know for those who struggle with the bondage of berating themselves, it can be a very complex, addictive habit. For further study, please look into Israel's blog: "Conviction vs. Condemnation?" at christianworldview.net/blog.

**Hormones:** Now don't any of you men start singing "I like being a guy . . ." or some of us women just might scream! Really, ladies, we have a unique challenge with hormones, and the resulting mood swings that often accompany them. A lot could be said about good nutrition and medical help if hormone levels are less than ideal. However, I want to focus primarily on simply recognizing that those times of the month, or postpartum, when hormones are going whacky, are going to be a bit more trying than usual, to say the least. Realize ahead of time that certain days, hormonally, may trigger anger for you. The key is doing all in your power *not* to pull the trigger and let anger fly.

Some women recognize that these times of the month are not good times for making any kind of long-term plans. Emotionally, they just feel fried and empty. Do yourself a favor if you struggle with this, and pre-determine not to let yourself make long-term relational choices with your family. If you have a mouthy teenager, this is probably not a good time to engage him or her in a disagreement. Wait just a few days until you are on an even keel. If you have youngsters that get into mischief, switch up your schedule and spend a lot of time reading aloud together. The fact is, we're going to have days when we're just feeling out of sorts, or maybe even down and out with hormonal issues. Anger will overtake us if we allow it to, but looking ahead to those challenging days and making the best of them (riding out the time before we need to deal with anything really serious if possible) can go a long way to keeping peace in our families.

I've never really had a grasp on the meaning of the passage in 1 Timothy where Paul gives this instruction: "Yet she will be saved through childbearing — if they continue in faith and love and holiness, with self-control" (1 Tim. 2:15). Whatever the promise there about the childbearing, this verse holds rich guidance about how to live out motherhood. We are to "continue in faith and love and holiness, with self-control." This is to be the earmark of our motherhood. When the tough days descend on you, don't lose heart. Keep on and continue in the good work of Christ-centered motherhood. It will reap fruit in time.

**Illness and Physical Limitations:** When illness and physical limitations make an unwelcome appearance in our homes, stress tries to barge in right behind. Simple tasks that used to be routine are now laden with complications. Where we used to have a bit of elastic to roll with the punches, illness brings along its own set of confining emotions that make caring for a family extra difficult. If sickness has you hostage right now, recognize that your emotions can get out of balance with the pain and unknown future. You may be irritated more quickly than usual but, even in your weakness, God wants to show Himself powerful. Don't thwart that by allowing anger to take up residence in your home.

**Special Needs Children:** Sometimes God sends parents gifts that are more challenging. Youngsters with mental or physical disabilities often expose many character flaws in their parents. The unique, and often repetitive, needs of a special needs child call for many sleepless nights, perseverance in the face of unrewarding work, and a great deal of patience. Yet, these needy ones are a gift from God. They are meant to help love abound and patience be perfected. If this is you, yours is definitely a challenging road, but you will also find much rich treasure along the way.

*Brook:* **Unhappiness:** The last anger trigger I want to look at in this chapter is unhappiness. Remember the old saying, "If Mama ain't happy, ain't *nobody* happy"? Mom's unhappiness directly opens the door for anger to come and roost in her life.

Unhappiness can be an elusive, mysterious malady, sometimes seeming to have no particular beginning or end. Other times, the source of unhappiness can have very specific roots that need dealt with head-on. There is no way we could possibly cover every aspect of unhappiness. However, it is important to recognize that we sometimes allow certain things or attitudes into our lives that only set us up for an angry mentality.

Mothering in our current culture is like a fish swimming upstream. Our neighbors, friends, aunts, and mothers often tell us women we need to find our real identity and self-worth outside of the realm of motherhood. While her children are under her care, a mother's calling is to be there for the nurture and training of her offspring. She might include many other responsibilities and services to others in her life, but to the best of her ability, the wise mother will be available during her children's growing-up years. It is the eternal investment in her children that will stand the real test of time, more than the pursuit of acclaim in the business or service, or even ministry arenas ever could.

Yet because of the loud voices about her, mothers can feel confused as to just what is worthwhile for her to put her hand to. In addition, when some of the ordinary days of motherhood settle on her — the days that aren't so full of glamor, or fun, or even variety — it can be easy for a mom to lose sense of the importance of her job. Sometimes moms feel like they do the same things, day in and day out, without seeing any amazing results. They feel like the world about them hustles and bustles with the significant, and they are stuck serving peanut butter and jelly sandwiches, and cleaning up spilled apple juice. Thus, unhappiness.

Unhappiness has its root in thinking that we should have something different than the life in front of us. If you find your heart longing for an escape from the "daily grind" of caring for a family, you will miss out on one of the greatest opportunities to really do something for God. Contentment comes as we walk in the place God has for us, unswerving in our trust that God will use every gift and talent in our life as He so chooses. With a God who cares that much for us, there can be no room for unhappiness to direct our steps.

### Questions to Consider

We want to encourage you to make a list, right now, before you go onto the next chapter, of four areas you recognize as anger triggers in *your* life. Perhaps it is something we brought up in this chapter, or maybe it is another topic altogether. If you can, nail down your own personal anger triggers to the most specific areas. Is it a cluttered home? Or is it that the children won't do their chores? Is it mealtime in general? Or more specifically, getting help washing the dishes? Is there anything you *can* do about that anger trigger? Is there anything you *should* do? (And, *no*, you can't list the names of your spouse or children as your anger triggers!) Once you have your list — pray!

On the flip side, sometimes positive habits can trigger in us a reminder to do what is right. What are some Scriptures that would help you remember to replace anger with patience? Where could you post these reminders so that they are sure to be a help to you?

Identifying your anger triggers can help you to identify in advance areas of your life that you can, and should, change to avoid stress and angry outbursts.

# 6
# Yelling Moms, Hollering Dads

## *Is Yelling Okay?*

Now and then, it actually seems like anger can bring about good results in the behavior of our children. We yell a bit, give a little display of emotion, and children seem to perk up for once and *listen*! And when they do, roused by volume and threats, something happens in a parent's brain that says, "See? It worked!"

Yelling is an easy practice to take up, and a very difficult habit to lie down. Somewhere in every parent's experience comes a time when little Johnny refuses to listen to a simple, kindly spoken command. So we instinctively try saying it again, only a little louder. And upon still receiving no response, our fire is kindled, and we increase the volume. Come on — you've done it, I've done it. Sure, there are times when a child legitimately can't hear, and the volume needs raised just a touch, but that's not what I'm referring to here. I'm talking about when our children can hear the words spoken and yet refuse to acknowledge. It is precisely at such a time that parents get this odd notion that repeating themselves in a louder and more authoritative voice will get the desired response.

It might . . . for a short time. But typically what happens is that Mom and Dad just have to now maintain the volume and angst at this high level to get any sort of attention at all in the future. Even the little tykes quickly figure out the game and learn that they aren't expected to listen until Mom and Dad's volume reaches a certain decibel and duration. If this is the case in your home, we'd like to suggest that you have actually trained your children to ignore you *until* such time as you are angry. This may not be the way you want it to be (maybe you even hate the anger that feels like a ball and chain), but it just seems like you are pulling teeth to get your children to do the basics in life, and even that feels like a battle.

We want to challenge you to stop battling your children. They aren't the enemy. Parents who combat their children by stooping to bicker with them or yell at them, have lost before they have even begun. Children aren't going to receive any help toward overcoming the weaknesses and foolishness endemic to the human race by a ranting, raving, raging mom or dad. Your children need you to step out of hollering mode.

But here's why that is easier said than done. When a parent hollers, stomps around, and yells, something happens in the parent's brain — like a chemical release. When a parent has said his or her piece, and gotten the irritation out of their system through yelling, their brain tells them that the situation is now under control, and it floods them with a sense of resolution and calm. Thus, yelling can become terribly addictive for parents. It feels like a fast track to getting their children's attention, and it leaves them feeling satisfied.

In fact, temporarily, yelling can go so well in a family that it seems justified. See if you haven't heard some of these, or even said some of these things:

"We're just a loud family — we like it that way! After all, it's our cultural heritage!"

"Oh, my kids know I don't really mean anything by making a little noise."

"Yelling is okay as long as you don't say anything nasty."

"Yelling is my children's cue that I really mean business."

And again: "At least my kids listen when I holler. It's the only thing that gets their attention. They know deep inside that I love them."

### For the Sake of the Children

So let's think about the children in these situations. Do they feel satisfied after a parent's yelling spree? Do they feel calmed? If you were in their shoes, would you feel like you had a renewed desire to do right in the future? Would you feel like even trying?

A child gains nothing by a parent's explosive temper. With that in mind, I ask you to step back from your life for a few minutes, hopefully while all is calm in your home, and really consider what it is you wish to accomplish in your home by giving way to yelling. Is it for your child's sake that you yell? Or your own?

Even if the words used are appropriate (no cursing, name calling, belittling, shaming), the atmosphere that volume alone sets is one of aggression and tension. For the parent, increasing the decibels fuels an attacking mode that rarely stays within the confines of appropriate words. When you attack people verbally, it automatically triggers their defense mechanism. Their walls go up, and they immediately begin forming both a defensive posture and a verbal defense. This creates an adversarial standoff that is not conducive to reconciliation and problem solving.

If the common passerby were to eavesdrop on your heated verbal barrage toward your child, would they see your heart of love drawing your child to repentance through witnessing your exchange . . . or would it leave them confused?

Children, big and small, sometimes seem to have an indomitable stubborn streak. It is human nature to want to eradicate that ugly thing we see in our children by using volume. Or we seek to match our children's stubborn streak with our own stubborn streak — which only leads to a power struggle.

Are you hoping to see your child brought low to examine wrongdoing in their life or to feel shame for some misdemeanor? Is this the only parenting technique that has seemed to work in your life? Would these techniques work in your life if friends and family were to treat you in the same way?

Galatians 5:17 sheds some light on this topic: "For the desires of the flesh are against the Spirit, and the desires of the Spirit are against the flesh, for these are opposed to each other, to keep you from doing the things you want to do." Anger, yelling, and bitterness are near and dear to our flesh. But they do not bring results in keeping with faith in Christ (see James 1:20).

The Book of Colossians lays it hard on us about these fleshly habits.

Put to death therefore what is earthly in you: sexual immorality, impurity, *passion*, evil desire, and covetousness, which is idolatry. On account of these the wrath of God is coming. In these you too once walked, when you were living in them. But now you must put them all away: anger, wrath, malice, slander, and obscene talk from your mouth. Do not lie to one another, seeing that you have put off the old self with its *practices* and have *put on* the new self, which is being renewed in knowledge after the image of its creator" (Col. 3:5–10, emphasis added).

The Creator lovingly brings us the consequences, discipline, and teaching we need in our lives to walk in purity and holiness. Can we do less for our children and expect good results?

### Be Willing to Consider Outside Assessment

Because of the fact that our hearts are so deceitful (Jer. 17:9), and it's so easy to lie to ourselves, we need to be willing to listen to what others have to say about our tendencies. A friend of ours recently told us that his younger teen daughter said, "Dad, you yell at me all the time." His initial reaction was to insist that he did not. In fact, in his mind, he doesn't really yell much at all. But his daughter was insistent. "All the time, Dad! You are always yelling." It is a good idea to listen to our spouses and our children on these matters, because they don't have a vested interest in defending our bad behavior (as we usually do!). Even if we aren't yelling or getting angry as often as they feel we are, the fact that they are still internalizing our frustration, and interpreting it as anger, means that our relationship is going in the wrong direction.

### But If I Don't Yell . . . They Won't Listen!

At first blush, this seems adamantly true. Children and young people who have become accustomed to Mom and Dad's raised voices tend to only heed when, well, the volume is turned up.

Unless your child has a true hearing condition, things can change. For the better!

*Brook:* Years ago when I was a young person, I worked on a volunteer basis as a pianist for our church's children's choir. There were approximately 40 energetic youngsters between the ages of five and eight. The children's choir director, Mrs. D., did a masterful job leading the group through rehearsal, then through a snack and craft time, then back for a few more minutes of singing. I hadn't noticed that the success of keeping so many bouncing boys and girls in tow was her calm, authoritative manner. That is, until one day during the craft time, she had to step out of the room for a few minutes. Pandemonium started to set in! The hum of 40 children talking raised and bounced off the ceiling. Crayons started to fly as boys played darts with each other. Girls screamed and cried, and another boy began running circles around the room. I began frantically going from table to table, trying to calm the girls down and instruct the boys to stop. I looked a bit helplessly at the adult volunteers standing on the sidelines watching the whole scene.

Then it suddenly went dark. There were no windows in the room, so when the lights were switched off, it was really black. Mrs. D's voice rang out firm but kind and "quiet." She flipped the lights back on and calmly told the children to take their seats. She informed them that this behavior was unacceptable. I couldn't believe it as those children dutifully found their seats and quieted down without a word.

It is important that we don't confuse the important role of godly leadership and authority parents hold with yelling, angry control. The issue is authority, not volume.

### Yelling Is the New Training Tool

These days, parents are fed so many confusing and contradictory beliefs from all sides about child rearing that it is no wonder we don't know what to do. Far too many of our generation grew up without seeing good parenting practices lived out in close proximity. With few reliable parenting tools available, yelling seems to be the one and only last resort. So many are doing it that we can even feel "all right" about ourselves for being yellers — because, well, everyone is doing it.

The atmosphere yelling creates promotes breaking a child's spirit. It wears on a body to be spoken to harshly and in an unduly loud voice. As soon as Mom or Dad's voice goes up, a child's defenses go up as well. Yelling does the exact opposite of what a Christian parent wants to see happen in their child. Instead of drawing that child closer to seeing the issue at hand, they are pushed away from receiving your word.

If you are a yeller, please realize our heart goes out to you. Our intention is to help us all look at this situation of anger and yelling and assess what it is really doing in us *and* our child. We've got to see clearly the damage an ongoing lifestyle of anger is causing. Only then will we see the desperate need we have for God to do a work in us. We know this can be a distressing topic. We've known so many moms and dads who feel so despairing of the anger that seems to control them. They hate the anger that overtakes them. It is like a cage that closes them in, never letting them go from its grips. Anger is suffocating for all involved. Look at these words:

> But we have this treasure in jars of clay, to show that the surpassing power belongs to God and not to us. We are afflicted in every way, but not crushed; perplexed, but not driven to despair; persecuted, but not forsaken; struck down, but not destroyed; always carrying in the body the death of Jesus, so that the life of Jesus may also be manifested in our bodies. For we who live are always

being given over to death for Jesus' sake, so that the life of Jesus also may be manifested in our mortal flesh" (2 Cor. 4:7–11).

But he said to me, "My grace is sufficient for you, for my power is made perfect in weakness." Therefore I will boast all the more gladly of my weaknesses, so that the power of Christ may rest upon me (2 Cor. 12:9).

Where do we get that grace? "But he gives more grace. Therefore it says, 'God opposes the proud, but gives grace to the humble' " (James 4:6; see also Phil. 1:6).

Breaking free from the grips of anger starts with softening our hearts.

Here are some significant steps to take to break the habit of yelling:

1. Make a plan ahead of time what you want to do differently next time you feel like raising your voice. Do the opposite of your instinct and talk very quietly. You are re-training yourself to control your volume by doing this.

2. Be near your child. It is really hard to holler at someone you are a foot away from.

3. Save yelling for times of immediate danger. ("Stop running into the street!")

4. Stop yourself if you find yourself yelling. If you need to take five minutes in a separate room, do it.

5. If your child is disobedient, address it right away. If you find that you are repeating your instructions frequently, it is because you are not following through with your commands, ensuring that they are followed. Constantly repeating yourself will lead to frustration.

6. If your children are old enough to read, write down your instructions for them. You'll probably be more concise that way, and this can be useful as you reset old patterns. Children need to know what is required of them, and having their responsibilities in writing often removes the "forgetting" factor, or the "I didn't know that" excuse.

7. Repent to your kids when you blow it. They know losing your cool isn't very mature, but it can do them a world of good to hear you acknowledge that.

"But what comes out of the mouth proceeds from the heart, and this defiles a person" (Matt. 15:18). We get so used to talking to our families that we can forget the tremendous weight the Lord puts on what comes out of our mouths. If there is anger coming out of our mouths, the Bible indicates this is a heart problem. Oftentimes, we think it is our children who need to be corrected, but sometimes, we need it even more! That reminds me of something Jesus said about a log and a speck in one's eye (see Luke 6:42).

### Who Is in Control?

One thing to remember is that when you have lost your control in an argument, it means that someone else has it. This is not an ideal scenario, especially when we are talking about our relationship with our children. Teenagers especially can push buttons, and if you aren't careful, you will find yourself on their level, having a good ole-fashioned squabble with your own child! You don't want to be dragged down to their level. You are the parent. They are the child. Don't allow them to be in the driver's seat of the conversation. When you are out of sorts, they have you exactly where they want you. Rein it in and be respectful. If you want respect, you can't act like a child.

### Anger Tears Down Relationships

If you are reading this book, we trust that your heart is toward your children, and you truly want to love them and see them grow in the Lord. Thus, it should go without saying that everything within you that tears down that relationship needs to be eliminated.

### Don't Undo What You Want to Build

Proverbs 14:1 jumps to the heart of the matter: "The wisest of women builds her house, but folly with her own hands tears it down." It is just plain foolish to carelessly toss aside wisdom during our children's young years by allowing anger to have a foothold in us.

Children reared in anger tend to go one of two ways. Either they will take on an aggressive, angry bitterness of their own, or they will retreat to a person or persons who will embrace them. But for the grace of God! The grace of God can change you from who you are today, to a person full of power in the Spirit to love others to Christ. Even if your children have long ago rejected you because of anger sowed in their youth, even if there seems no hope for change in your relationship with them, God wants to use your repentance on this issue.

### Further Fruits of Yelling

There are few things more painful than seeing our own faults mirrored in the lives of our children. Oh, the pain of it all when we see our children yelling, hollering, and angrily barking at each other! As we've mentioned before, yelling can seem to bear some good fruit for a season, but when it has grown, it becomes evident that the fruit is rotten. If you hear your own anger reflected in the lives of your children, don't throw up your hands in despair. Seeing it and recognizing its source is a mercy of God, even if painful. It is never too late to see what the power of God can do in your family.

On a practical note, your child's anger needs to be addressed, yes, by imperfect you. If your child/children aren't yet fully aware of your repentance in your anger toward them and that you are seeking to change your ways, then that is your first step. Be open about what God is doing in your life to help you overcome anger.

While a child's anger directed at his sibling is hard enough to take, your child's anger toward you may be even harder to handle. If your child is so frustrated that he or she is lashing out in anger toward you, you need to begin a process of winning back their hearts. You need to lovingly establish (or reestablish) proper boundaries that have been missing. You need to pray and seek God regarding what you have done in the past to lose your child's respect, and what you can do to regain that trust and honor that you need to have from your child. This process may involve inviting your church elders, or a qualified biblical counselor into the equation, to help you identify where things have broken down and what you can do to regain your child's heart.

## Be Careful How Your Words Define Your Child

> Let no corrupting talk come out of your mouths, but only such as is good for building up, as fits the occasion, that it may give grace to those who hear (Eph. 4:29).

> The good person out of the good treasure of his heart produces good, and the evil person out of his evil treasure produces evil, for out of the abundance of the heart his mouth speaks (Luke 6:45).

We've mentioned this passage before, but it is such an important one, that we want to repeat it here. If our hearts hold the "good treasure" of desiring to see our children grow in faith in God, then the abundance of our words will always come back around to promoting faith in God. But if we reserve an angry and critical attitude toward our children, that "evil treasure" in our hearts will come out in our speech. We address this in more detail in the chapter "The Power of Affirmation."

### Value Your Own Words

One of the ways we cultivate yelling in our lives, particularly with our children, is that we ourselves don't take our words seriously. It is quite natural for a parent to have their ire stirred when their child doesn't care to listen. Somehow we need to get it through our thick heads that if a child won't listen the first time, saying it louder, and with more emphasis, will not suddenly make a difference. True, it might in the short term, but let us say this straightforwardly: you will ultimately lose their hearts. We've seen it happen over and over. If anger and hollering are a way of life for you, get off that track as fast as possible, because the end thereof leads to death in the relationship.

The fact is, all of us have important things to pass on to our children. We have deep, eternal truths stamped on our hearts that we want to communicate to our children. We have Scriptures that bear directly on life decisions we are making with our families that we need to share. We have practical words of advice to pass on from our own experiences in the school of hard knocks. Our words are important. They hold wealth for our children if they can only stop and listen.

We build that "listenership" with them when they are young. And, like all children, they'll test you. On a whim, they'll see how important it is and act like you never said a word. Too many times, parents themselves don't value their own words enough to make sure that they follow through and insist on obedience. If you don't intend for your children to perform an action, don't bother to instruct them. If it is worth your time to tell them, then it is certainly worth your time to follow up and ensure that they have followed through.

It really isn't ultimately about picking up the toys, or coming for peanut butter and jelly sandwiches — it is about building a relationship with them that will eventually be a conduit for the Word of the Lord to take root in their hearts.

Teddy Roosevelt once famously said, in regard to government: "Speak softly and carry a big stick." If your children aren't listening to you, anger and yelling aren't the key. Make sure you follow up all disobedience with appropriate discipline, and when possible, allow natural consequences to come to bear on the situation. The more closely related the consequences, the better.

As an example, one of our children just last night procrastinated during kitchen cleanup after dinner. When it was time for a family movie, this child went in and sat down to watch the film with everyone else. We could have decided to "pitch a fit" about this behavior, but instead, we calmly walked the child into the kitchen and reminded them that the dishwasher had to be full and running before movie watching could commence. The child missed the first 15 minutes of the movie doing something that could have been done earlier.

### The Power of Praise

There is so much to say about the power of praise on behalf of our children. But I want to point out that the very act of giving praise can have an incredible benefit for recalibrating the heart of a parent.

Our words hold such power. In a minor way, as we reflect the Creator in the awesomeness of His power in words (who else speaks a universe into existence!), our own words are a powerful force for molding and forming relationships. Jesus said, "It is the Spirit who gives life; the flesh is no help at all. The words that I have spoken to you are spirit and life" (John 6:63). As we follow after Jesus' pattern and speak words of life and spirit to our children, we make less and less room for words of the flesh (our anger!) and death (to the relationship).

Perhaps you've reached a place in the relationship with your child that there just isn't anything good to say. I mean, as a mom or dad, you've been there for the good, the *bad*, and the *ugly*. When all that comes to your mind to speak are angry, biting words, check yourself. Jesus found a way to bring words that brought life and spirit — words spoken to a blind people living in darkness and rebellion. Even when our children walk in ways that incite our anger, we must be looking for ways to bring a healing light, a path of hope, a hand toward walking in righteousness. This is presenting the gospel of grace — there is hope for the wayward sinner! And in offering this kind of love and patience, something happens in our hearts. We're softened. Not toward sin, but toward the sinner.

### Questions to Consider

Parenting is about sowing and reaping. What fruit will grow from seeds of anger?

What are the negative effects you've seen in your children from anger?

What are two situations you are dealing with right now where you feel your children won't listen? Has raising your voice helped? What is a better long-term solution?

# 7

# "But I'm Not Patient!"

### Staring Down My Anger

*Brook:* I'll never forget the fateful day that my own anger stared me in the face. Growing up, I never struggled with anger, or even with having an attitude. I naively thought it had something to do with my studied respect for character. But I was about to have that overturned!

You see, even though I thought of myself as an easygoing person, I had never stood up to the rigors of parenting. That is, until I had children. Now, I'm going to guess that many of you are in the same boat, but I didn't just get a child for a firstborn — I got a lawyer. I wish someone would have told me that most firstborns turn from those loveable, cuddly babies to hard-core, professional lawyers at the ripe old age of two. I was aghast that one so young could have the debating and reasoning abilities to put an adult on the defense! I was constantly justifying commonly held beliefs, like "yes, vegetables are good for you, donuts are not," and the like. I wouldn't have believed it by hearsay, but it happened in my own house. I love firstborns. They have so much determination, and often are natural-born leaders. I've learned a lot since then about the fruitlessness of arguing with a toddler, but as a young mom, I was blown away by the little legal tyrant.

On this particular day, my toddler-turned-five-year-old had a plan in his mind about exactly what his day should hold. He was more than convinced that he had the moral stability and wise judgment to manage his own day, aside from his mother's direction.

So began our conversation. After duly informing him that, no, he could not skip his vegetables and eat donuts, and, no, he could not go outside to play until the little ones were up from their naps, the lawyer in him sought to bring to light every aspect his little brain could produce to present why his plan was good and his mother's oversight was unnecessary. With a final "no," I turned back to my dishpan of soaking dishes . . . when he started up again.

So I said it: "*You* are about to *make me* lose my. . . ." I meant to say "patience" or "temper," but I choked! I knew in reality the blame for my losing my patience didn't rest with my son. It was entirely my own responsibility. Now, obviously a lot could be said here about training, but that is outside the scope of this book. (Look into Israel's book, chock full of biblical guidance on child training, *Full Time Parenting: A Guide to Family-Based Discipleship.*) But I was a young mom, quite new to the job. Let me just suffice it to say, I have a tender heart toward young moms. So many of us come to this amazing job with a lot of heart but little, if any, experience, and often with very few living examples of good parenting.

So I stood there, dishwater dripping off my hands onto the kitchen floor, aware for the first time in my life just how lacking I was in patience. Since then, I've talked with a lot of moms, and I can identify with so many of these sweet-natured moms. We didn't even know we could be angry or impatient until these little youngsters entered our lives.

### Button Pushers Reveal What's Inside

The scariest thing to realize was that my little button pusher only revealed what was inside of me. Yes, that sweet little lawyer needed training, but I also had to face the fact that, when "bumped," ugly things had been revealed. In my easygoing youth, with less responsibility, I just hadn't really been tried. Now I had four little ones doing their God-given duty to wake me up for midnight feedings, wake me up at the crack of dawn, ask for food, more food, and more food (and dump it off the highchair just for good measure!).

I had a little one testing out every boundary just to see who really was the mom around here anyway. Oh, those years were exhausting, but I praise God for my little button pushers. God used them to help expose my heart. Had it not been for them, I would have never seen my desperate need for God to work out His patience in me. My life before this was too simple and carefree, and I was usually able, in my own strength, to squelch any impatience. Without these little ones tugging and pulling on my emotions and will, I would never have started on a journey (that I'm still on!) to find out how to get the patience of Christ's Spirit inside me.

God designs and specifically sends each of our children to us — uniquely tailored to push our buttons. My children wouldn't have the same effect on you, nor yours on me. God knew just what each of us would need, and He matched you up with your children for the express purpose of giving you a little bit more than you could chew. An ancient Indian proverb says, "Whatever you are overflowing with will spill out when you are bumped." This concept takes on a whole new depth in parenting.

Amy Carmichael, in her book *Candles in the Dark*, puts it this way: "A cup brimful of sweetness cannot spill even one drop of bitter water, no matter how suddenly jarred."[1]

When ugly things pour out of us, it is so easy to blame someone, or at least some*thing*. Yet Scripture is clear that "The good person out of the good treasure of his heart produces good, and the evil person out of his

---

1. Amy Carmichael, *Candles in the Dark* (Ft. Washington, PA: Christian Literature Crusade, 1982).

evil treasure produces evil, for out of the abundance of the heart his mouth speaks" (Luke 6:45).

### Patience: A Sliding Scale?

My journey started when I began to examine patience in light of its quality as a fruit of the Spirit. Honestly, patience, up to this point in my life, had been more of the self-restraint model. I kept myself in check because I required it of myself. But when I came to grips with the fact that I didn't have enough patience for this mothering "thing," I knew I didn't have what it was going to take for the long haul.

So I began pondering that statement we sometimes flippantly make: "You are about to make me lose my patience!" or "I'm losing my patience/temper!" We act like patience comes on a scale of 1–10. If you are a very patient person, perhaps you score way high, like a 7, 8, or even a 9. But, if bumped, it might sink way down low, to like a 4. If you don't watch it, it may even sink as far as a 3 or a 2. And, wow, if someone irritates you, and it gets to 1 or a 0 — what then?

So let me ask you a question: What does patience bring forth when it is tested?

As I studied patience, I began to see that it is an outworking of being indwelt by the Holy Spirit. This is the powerful Spirit of God, who isn't fazed by a few naughty children or an angry teenager or an over-the-top bad day. I needed that kind of patience. I realized this kind of patience didn't have a sliding scale. Either I was making room in my life for the Spirit to lead me, or I wasn't. Either I was walking in patience from God, or I wasn't.

I realized that patience — I mean the patience born of the Spirit that Galatians 5 speaks about — will only bring forth more patience when it is tried and tested.

How can the Spirit bring forth anything not of the Spirit?

> My brethren, count it all joy when you fall
> into various trials, knowing that the testing of
> your faith produces patience. But let patience
> have its perfect work, that you may be perfect and
> complete, lacking nothing (James 1:2–4; NKJV).

I guess it has made me wonder how often we tend to label something we could more accurately call "temporary self-restraint" or "temporary peace" or "for the time being, I'm gentle" or "I'm tolerating this as long as I can endure it" . . . as *patience*. If "patience" that is tested results in a diminishment of patience, then perhaps we never started with patience at all, but a phony put-on attitude we just call "patience."

The good news is that patience is something of the Spirit of God. It is something He Himself will bear in us. Too often, we view the fruits of the Spirit listed in Galatians (5:22–23) as a checklist of good ideas to strive for and acquire, when the reality is, we haven't the slightest ability to manufacture these fruits in and of ourselves any more than we could grow a real apple off of our fingertips. The genuine article of patience must be borne solely and only by the Holy Spirit within us.

That doesn't mean you can just sit back and wait for this precious fruit to just grow on its own. It is our abiding in Jesus that will bear the fruit of patience (see John 15). He is sure to provide the lessons we need in patience if we are willing to make good use of them. Masking our irritations and displeasure with a facade that is genteel and laid back won't produce patience. Patience that is of the Spirit, when tested, will only bring forth more patience. Let me say it again, a "patience" that wears out can't be patience of the Lord Jesus. He says in John 15:16, "You did not choose me, but I chose you and appointed you so that you might go and bear fruit — fruit that will last" (NIV). True patience is a fruit that will last.

This fruit that Jesus talks about has a purpose to fulfill. Just as an apple farmer would never intend to grow an orchard without a purpose, our gardener intends the fruit He grows in our lives to fulfill His purposes, one of which is to reach into the lives of those around us.

Patience goes beyond personal victory (I didn't lose my temper today) to reach deeply into our relationships with others, which is where the real action of Spirit-filled living takes place. In other words, we'd probably all think we're perfectly patient if we lived alone on a desert island! In the real world of irritating people with annoying habits, problems, and downright difficult relationships, patience (again, we're talking about patience borne of the Holy Spirit) looks beyond ourselves to build others up in the Lord.

### Get off the Ladder and Turn Around!

I know, it sounds kinda platonic to just say, "Have the fruit of the Spirit of patience and self-control and all your troubles will be over."

Patience simply doesn't come by grit. It is not an attitude of "I will, I *will*, I WILL have patience!" It truly is something that God does in us. Does that mean we give up trying? Does it mean we roll over like a dead dog? Of course not! It means we rely all the harder on the God who helps us say no to sin. "For the grace of God has appeared, bringing salvation to all people, training us to renounce ungodliness and worldly passions, and to live self-controlled, upright, and godly lives in the present age" (Titus 2:11–12). This training is a work God wants to do in us — helping us to live self-controlled lives!

Making room for the Spirit of God to live in us is key.

A second way that the "sliding scale" of patience hinders us is that we also view reclaiming self-controlled living as something we achieve rung by rung, as if climbing a ladder. We view becoming angry, or hollering at our children, or losing our temper as "falling off the ladder." We feel terrible about it and may even berate ourselves, viewing regaining self-control as now a long ways off — something difficult to attain, only achieved after years of hard work. That might be true if we were talking about merely putting a cap on your behavior and being willing to be patient. But I'm talking about abiding in the Spirit of the living God so that you are walking in His patience and self-control. The fruits of the Spirit are for those walking in the Spirit. The lusts of the flesh are for those walking after the flesh.

> But I say, walk by the Spirit, and you will not gratify the desires of the flesh (Gal. 5:16).

When you fail (sadly, it will happen), instead of falling into a muddle over it . . . repent. Yes, right where you are. Invite fellowship with the Lord again and get going, back in the midst of life. We fail, not because we have such difficult and demanding children, or because we just didn't bite our tongues hard enough. We fail because we stopped, somewhere along the line, abiding in the Lord Jesus. The key is to get back to walking with the Lord as quickly as possible.

### I Just Don't Have Enough Patience!

I mentioned above that God specially designed your children with their own, uniquely installed irritation buttons — with you in mind! Now this great God is good and kind; it wasn't really to make life more difficult for you. It was to show your need for *Him*, and to draw you closer to Him. Let's face it. There is nothing like family life to push us to our knees! We are imperfect people, living among imperfect people.

Interestingly, a lot of what sets our blood boiling when it comes to our children is the fact that they are, well, just like us! They are like little mirrors that imitate all the weaknesses we'd rather no one see, and reflect our own shortcomings that we already dislike about ourselves. But praise God! This is for our sanctification!

I'll be the first to admit, this isn't easy. When these little mirrors show us ourselves, the easy road is to act like the man in James 1:23–24: "For if anyone is a hearer of the word and not a doer, he is like a man who looks intently at his natural face in a mirror. For he looks at himself and goes away and at once forgets what he was like."

When we encounter our own weaknesses reflected in our own little "mini me," the temptation is to find some escape. We may look for ways to be a part-time parent and relieve some of the responsibility. But it is precisely through more involvement with our children, not less, that God intends to refine *our* character. We often get so hyper-focused on the fact that our children need to grow up that we forget that God has a vested interest in this whole parenting journey you are on, and He wants to see *you* grow!

James goes on to say these words about the man who, seeing himself as he really is, acts on it: "But the one who looks into the perfect law, the law of liberty, and perseveres, being no hearer who forgets but a doer who acts, he will be blessed in his doing" (James 1:25).

### *If Your Vision Doesn't Scare You, It's Too Small*

It's a good thing most of us haven't the foggiest idea what parenting is all about before we get started or we'd be scared stiff! Parenting doesn't come in a nice tidy box that is contained, or that we necessarily feel adequate for. There will come a time for each of us, even the most capable, poised, patient parents, where we are driven to our knees. That's okay, because this is where God can minister grace to us.

The parenting process is going to test your patience. You will have many triggers to anger. Yet listen to this exchange between Corrie ten Boom and her father, Casper ten Boom, as recorded in *Casper ten Boom: God's Man*:

> When Mr. West left, I said to Father, "Mr. West had exactly the same [questions and doubts] as he had last week and two weeks ago. I think you have a lot of patience."
>
> "Girl, doesn't the Lord have a lot of patience with me and with you?"
>
> That evening I had difficulty in repairing a very small watch. Just when it was almost ready, I broke a part.
>
> "Papa, please help me. I have broken the balance of the watch."
>
> "You know there is nobody in the world I would rather help than my own daughter," was his kind answer.
>
> I had to go back to him three times. "I am so sorry, Papa, but I have broken it again!"
>
> "Give it to me. I will help you."
>
> "Papa, where did you get your patience?"

"Girl, we have a privileged job. There is nothing like watch repairing for learning patience. And don't forget that patience is a fruit of the Spirit."[2]

I am always amazed when I think of Casper ten Boom. Of all the vocations he could have chosen, he embraced the fact that watchmaking could teach him about patience. *That's* how highly he valued patience. I would add to this account that there is nothing like parenting to teach one patience. It is a tailor-made "job" to teach us self-control.

What would happen if we embraced this kind of perspective? What if we woke up excited about the specific, tailor-made lesson laid out before us, with ample opportunity to learn patience?

It is in God's heart for us to develop patience. As you examine your own life, don't say, "But I just haven't any patience!" As you abide in Him, He will take you through an amazing journey that will build this precious fruit of patience in you.

Maybe you didn't choose parenting for its superior quality in providing opportunities to learn patience. But here you are, enrolled in a class all your own, with the Master Teacher. Will you embrace the challenge in front of you?

### Questions to Consider

Do you view your button pushers as annoyances?

What needs to happen in your perspective before that could change?

In what ways have you viewed stresses as a curse, rather than an aid to your spiritual growth?

---

2. Corrie Ten Boom, *Father ten Boom: God's Man* (Old Tappan, NJ: Fleming H. Revell Co., 1978) p. 124–125.

# 8

# What Patience Is and Isn't

### *This Ain't Your Grandma's Patience!*

Throughout this book we've been delving into understanding anger and the need to remove it from parenting. We can look just about anywhere in our culture and see angry and stressed-out parenting — the park, the toy store, maybe even in our own homes. Anger in the parent-child relationship can often be fairly easy to identify. It isn't all that hard to see and know that the anger needs to go. But sometimes it can be a little harder to know exactly where we should be headed as parents. Our perception of patience is often a bit undefined, fuzzy, and thus hard to grasp. So let's take a look at what patience actually is and what it is not, so that we can get a better hold of where we want to be headed.

> *Brook:* Okay, I admit it. Sometimes the word "patience" sounds kinda dull to me. Does it to you too? When I picture patience, I think of a sweet, elderly grandma sitting in a rocking chair. I can just see her in my mind's eye: her folded hands resting in her lap; her serene, mild smile; her unwrinkled brow. If her little grandchildren or, for that matter, great-grandchildren should run up to her with their little trials and sorrows, she would be the picture of patience in calmly hearing them out and gently comforting them. I love it! I hope to be that grandma someday. But I don't like being locked into thinking this is what patience looks like, because, well, I don't live there. I live in a houseful of children, some quite young. My hands are never resting in my lap, because, at our house, there are things like dirty dishes and piles of laundry and muddy boots making tracks on the floor.
>
> When I think of patience as that grandma, I almost get frustrated! Sure, it would be halfway easy to be relaxed and patient if I had not a care or responsibility in the world! What about patience for people living busy

(maybe even over-the-top busy) lives with irritations that drive them nuts?

At other times, I picture patience much like the lovely plaques sold at Christian bookstores. They are so very pretty. Most of the time there is a painting or photo of an inviting meadow, sprinkled with daisies. Little white butterflies gracefully hover here and there, the sky is blue, the sun is shining. And plastered above in decorative script, the word "patience" puts in our mind what this scene should invoke. Don't get me wrong, the view is beautiful. I love meadows and butterflies and scripty fonts. But when I'm standing in my kitchen, staring down at spilled milk for the second time that morning, recovering from a headache and a youngster determined to test boundaries, that picture and what it represents might as well be a million miles away. I don't know if that lovely plaque is supposed to provide a momentary escape or show me a place of refuge, but this also is not where I live. And I'm assuming for most of you in the adventurous season of parenting, this is not where you live either.

### Patience Isn't Passive

I believe one of the faulty ways we view patience is that we think it is passive. For those Type A folks, or those with a more demonstrative personality, it is all the more important to realize that patience is not wimpy. Passivity calls for inaction, refraining from getting involved. Patience is neither, but is reflective rather of *how* one acts, how one is involved.

Patience is an *active* choice to walk, not in a demanding, controlling, and angry manner toward those around us but, instead, with enduring love and encouragement.

But thou, O man of God, flee these things; and follow after righteousness, godliness, faith, love, patience, meekness (1 Tim. 6:11; KJV).

We are commanded to actively run away from fleshly desires and actively pursue the things that are good for our soul. You can't stand still. You will always be running away from something and into something else.

### Patience Is Not a Pushover

Patience does not overlook sin.

Patience does not enable bad behavior.

Patience does not have a martyr's attitude.

True patience is not wimpy — trying to appease others and just being quiet. There is a time to speak up with the truth, yet it can be done with love and patience.

Patience isn't always pretty. Sometimes it even confronts the bad behavior of another. Always out of love, of course, persevering with someone else till they reach victory in an area that has held them down.

### Patience Is Not Blind (Does Not Hide Sin)

Patience of the Spirit doesn't give up on pointing others to walk with the Lord. It doesn't give up on people for personal grievances or irritations.

Patience is not uncaring. True patience is not taking an "I don't care" attitude or a "what will be, will be" attitude. Other people will fail us, and it is no sin to call another's wrong what it is: wrong. But when that time comes, each of us has a choice to make in our response. It is all too easy for us to respond to another's *fleshly* attitudes with *fleshly* attitudes of our own. Our natural response is to look at ourselves in the process — what was done to *me* — and allow the situation to steal our peace.

Yet a different approach is to bear with the weaknesses of another and to support that person to grow in Jesus. Patience may take on overlooking another's weaknesses, but it also may include gently persevering with another to help him or her mature. A mother may sweetly (patiently) tell her child to pick up his dirty socks ten times a day to no avail. In one sense we might applaud her for not "losing her cool," which, of course, is right, but if her "patience" enables her child to ignore authority, is she really helping her child to grow in what is right?

Patience needs to extend beyond our own hearts to build up others compassionately. We've got to get it out of our heads that patience is sugary-sappy sweetness. Yes, it is sweet, but patiently walking with someone requires speaking the truth *with* love. I like to think of it as coming alongside others, putting your arm around them, and helping them walk toward Jesus.

Patience cares so deeply for another's soul that it doesn't turn a blind eye to the needs of that soul. "Rather, speaking the truth in love, we are to grow up in every way into him who is the head, into Christ" (Eph. 4:15). First Corinthians 13 teaches us that love is patient. If we want to have patience, we must have love.

### We Need a New Picture of Patience

**Brook:** When we take away false preconceptions that patience is some sort of weak, warm, fuzzy feeling of pretending, we're never ruffled; we're left with a need for a new picture of patience. I want to present three new pictures.

### Patience Is Like a Sword

Okay, so this isn't exactly what most of us have in mind when we think of gentle patience, but here is one way to look at it: patience is powerful. Its strong use, wielded like a sword, cuts out the anger, as well as the dissonance and rebellion. Think of Proverbs 15:1, which instructs us that, "A soft answer turns away wrath, but a harsh word stirs up anger." Do you know how strong wrath is? Yet a soft answer — a patient answer — has the power to turn it away. We need something like this in our homes.

Patience, a way of living by the Spirit, is also useful for putting to death the deeds of the body (anger, anyone?). "For if you live according to the flesh you will die, but if by the Spirit you put to death the deeds of the body, you will live" (Rom. 8:13). That really doesn't sound too wimpy!

### Patience Is Like a Door

Anger slams the "door" in the face of relationships. Anger and pride must be closely related, because anytime anger shows up, pride is right there, rooting it on. Anger in the family arena says, "I'm glad I'm not like *you*! I want to get away from *you* and have nothing to do with *you*." Anger stands off away from a person. Anger closes the door, puts up a wall. Patience, in contrast, opens the door of relationship. It says, "You may have done wrong, but I want to walk alongside you and encourage you to gain godly victory. I will persist in loving you to truth." The old-fashioned word for patience, "longsuffering," says it all.

Patience is welcoming our children into a safe place where truth is upheld, and where we will go to bat with them against any sin that would weigh them down.

### Patience Is Like a Fire

Many times I think something that hinders us is the false conception that patience is something one magically just attains one day — forever after that they are just "happily patient." In reality, it is something more akin to healthy eating. We can tell ourselves all day that we'll start on that diet as soon as life slows down, or that we can't eat nutritious meals because our life is so hectic. Or we might use the excuse for some unnecessary pounds by saying, "Well, I just have a sweet tooth." One day we might choose to eat well, but the next we give into temptation and eat a large double-cheese pizza and a pan of brownies. At what point does a person turn the tide and switch from junk food to nutritious meals? When they consistently refuse to give in to food cravings and desires, and instead act on intentional decisions. The same is true, to a great degree, with choosing patience over anger.

We're sad to report there is no magic "patience" pill that you can swallow that will just reduce your appetite for anger. The process to give up anger might be slow. It might be painful. The temptation to give into anger "just this once" may present itself to you every day for a very long time. But I am here to say that the power of choosing, day after day, the greater choice of nurture over anger will, in time, become a way of life. Patience is not an elusive quality only available to a select few on this earth. It is for you. It is for those who right now find themselves addicted to angry outbursts.

The glorious truth is that God is no respecter of persons. "If any of you lacks wisdom, let him ask God, who gives generously to all without reproach, and it will be given him" (James 1:5).

Patience (like anger) is like a fire in that it can start small and, with time and the right fuel, grow to be a mighty strength in our lives. Fire is a living thing, ever changing. The same is true with patience. It isn't a once-swallowed item that we now "have" in our possession, but rather something that can become a part of the core of who we are as we live life. Making that switch from anger to patience can be difficult. Maybe it won't even come out right at first. We need to stop being fearful about this patience thing and our inability to walk it out perfectly. You might fail and have to "relight" that fire of patience many times. In owning up to anger, we have to admit we aren't the perfect parents we would like to see ourselves as. But that patience, no matter how small, or how much it seems to flicker and wants to die out, is a force that is beautiful. With time, by God's grace, it can become a steady flame, then a fire that gives out warmth.

> **Brook:** Finally, I think of patience as a fire because of the warmth and light it gives. On a cold winter night, everyone is drawn toward the heat and glow of a fire. Its beauty is a joy to behold, and it cuts away at the chill in

the air. Just so, a person of patience draws others by the warmth and light. Anger sends someone away, giving them the "cold shoulder"; patience draws them close and gives.

### Questions to Consider

Which have you more frequently utilized: the sword of anger or the sword of patience?

What are ways you've slammed the "door" of relationship by angrily reacting to your child?

Does it scare you to think of patience as a fire — a living, breathing thing? Why or why not?

# 9

# Nurture in the Heart of Correcting

*Brook:* We've talked a lot about anger throughout this book, and the need for parents to put it far away from them in their relationship with their children. Of all the chapters in this book, this particular topic has to be one of my favorites. I love it, because I am experiencing the joy of going from what used to be the biggest anger trigger of all for me (correcting my children) to embracing a new approach that helps me stay calm, guide my child, and leave the situation being more closely bonded with that child.

### Replacing Anger with Something More Powerful

Before you get the false idea that I've got it all together, let me be quick to say that the contrasting lifestyles of anger are a choice. Temptation is not a choice, but acting on that temptation is something we choose. Over the last several years, as I have put into my life the principles in this chapter, I am thrilled to say that intentional choices toward patience and nurturing can become a way of life; however, I am ashamed to say that there have been days when I have chosen to give in to the temptation of anger.

During the course of writing this book, we came upon the very last warm days of summer. The weather was picture perfect, the sky cloudless, and yardwork was waiting. So I gathered up all my young people, we trooped outside, and we had a great time working on various outdoor projects . . . with tools . . . several tools. I don't know about your neck of the woods, but in our area, even cheap tools aren't too cheap.

While we worked, we talked about all kinds of things. That's the sort of thing you do on a perfect day outside. We talked about the old black-and-white reruns my children love, about fall coming and when

we would make applesauce, about the new science cur-
riculum we had just started. We just all around had a
great time.

Toward the end of our day, two boys were still finishing up their section, so I took everyone else inside to
start dinner. Between kitchen tasks, I checked on those
two as they finished up, reminding them to put the tools
away when they were done. Before long, I could spy
them out my window playing, so I went out to supervise
the clean-up task force. I called to different children,
directing various ones to pick up certain tools, and all
was well. I even came out a second time to double check
on the project, noted a few things left out, and again
directed. By this time the wind had picked up. and I
could see rain clouds rolling in.

Dinner was ready, and once again I asked my Teddy
Bear of a son if he had picked up the tools I had last
mentioned. "Yep!" came his cheerful reply. I knew some
of the tools were a bit hard to see among the grass, so
I listed them just to double check. Okay, all was well,
dinner dishes washed, a relaxing evening, and we all
went to bed.

Then came the rain. And it rained and it poured.
But guess what I found the next morning? Several tools
had sat out in the rain, all by their lonesome, all night
long! I was frustrated! I had spent so much time going
over and over that exact issue. I had made sure I did my
part to give clear directions, and even to follow up and
ask for a double check!

So, I ignored all the aspects of this chapter, the beautiful treasures that I have at other times put into practice. I immediately proceeded to chew out that Teddy
Bear about the tools, which were already showing rust
spots. I wasn't really eager to hear anything come out of

his mouth. I just liked the sound of my own voice yak-
king, so I made sure to speak up and ask three times in a
row just what he was thinking! Didn't he care about the
tools? Didn't he get what I had told him? Why didn't he
bother to listen?

My frustration was on a roll, and while I knew inside
it would be better to stop and salvage things now, I felt
I had a right to air out my frustration and let that guy
know that he had better not let that happen again.

I was too busy ranting to even listen to his quick and
sincere, "I'm sorry, Mama, I didn't see those tools."

Not long afterward, when my steam had just started
to cool, I knew I had not walked that situation out well.
I had done nothing in my conversation to truly correct
my son. Neither had I looked for ways to build him up
to do right the next time. I hadn't looked for any solutions, or even reached across to make sure my son knew
I loved him. I really just wanted to vent my irritation.
So I called my Teddy Bear and repented to him for my
stinky attitude. "I didn't need to have an attitude about
the tools. Next time I say go double check, you need to
go and do that. Or, if you can't find any more, ask someone to help you. But it was not right of me to be upset at
you." A long hug later, and all is well again.

### Replacing Anger with Nurture

Over the years, as I've sought to remove anger from life,
the area of calmly correcting my children has been the
biggest challenge. The change started for me when the
words of James 1:20 sank deep into my heart: "For the
anger of man does not produce the righteousness of
God." Oh! That's what I was going for: seeking to rein-
force God's righteousness in my children! Many times,
my anger was really an attempt to grasp at and force

righteousness on my children. But this Scripture is so clear: If I want to see God's righteousness in my young-sters, I had better not employ my human anger, which is a sure-fire way to miss His righteousness in their lives. God Himself is slow to anger, and this attribute is closely linked to His love. (See Ps. 145:8; Joel 2:13; Num. 14:18; and Ps. 86:15, among others.)

As I've taken this journey away from anger, I've seen the incredible importance (especially as it relates to cor-recting our children when they need it) to not merely eradicate anger, but to replace it. Jesus talked about the need to fill the heart with good, and not just leave it empty or devoid of evil (Luke 11:25). Just leaving anger out of our interactions with our children isn't enough. In order to reach deeply into their hearts with the trans-forming truth of the Word and holy living, we need to deliver it with patience. The word I like to use best here is "nurture." Noah Webster's 1828 Dictionary defines nurture as:

**NURTURE,** *noun*
1. That which nourishes; food; diet.
2. That which promotes growth; education; instruction.
   [Eph. 6:4]

**NURTURE,** *verb transitive*
1. To feed; to nourish.
2. To educate; to bring or train up.

He was nurtured where he was born.

### Nurture Opens the Door

Do you remember the "door" word picture of patience from the chapter, "What Patience Is and Isn't"? Anger is like slamming a door in a person's face. But nurture — a deep, kind interest in helping another grow — is like opening the door. Whereas a parent's anger leaves a child with a sour taste in his mouth, a parent's nurture promotes the softening of the heart.

### Walk in Repentance

Perhaps another way to describe that promotion of softening the heart is helping our child learn how to take the steps of repentance. Let's face it. Somewhere in the midst of raising those sweet, innocent babies, they grow up and have this odd and unnecessary desire to test the boundaries of normal, sane, healthy living. And sometimes they do it defiantly! Young children deliberately throw their food on the floor moments after you told them not to. A step older, and those same children sneak cookies out of the cookie jar and lie to cover it up. Teens take on sulky attitudes and react badly to being told they have boundaries. At some point, those sweet, angelic children of ours need corrected.

> *Brook:* My first several years as a mom weren't exactly successful. I saw the correction the little people needed, but didn't know how to deliver it in a way anyone, let alone a child, could receive. I feel for firstborns (perhaps because I am one?). They get to experience their parents' growing pains. I saw that, somehow or other, my children needed hearts that would hear me out when I needed to correct them, and receive it with repentance. I didn't know how to instill that in them, so I just started talking about it. We would talk about it when an issue came up, we would talk about it during a fine time on any old day, we read books about it that were way over their heads, and we memorized a little poem from the late 19th century:
>
>> Tis not enough to say
>> "I'm sorry" and repent
>> And still go on from day to day
>> Just as we always went.

Repentance is to leave
The sins we loved before
And show that we in earnest grieve
By doing them no more. — Anonymous

I don't really know if it made a lick of difference in their lives, but it sure did in mine. As I understood more what repentance was, and yearned to walk it out in my own life, as well as see genuine repentance in their lives, my approach to correcting changed. I began desiring to stop anything that built resistance in their hearts. I started calming down, slowing down, and focusing not just on pointing out what bad things needed to stop, but looking for ways that they could relate to what I was saying. I made up stories, once in a great while I found a movie that illustrated some point we had talked about, we sang applicable songs, I used humor. And something changed. Now, it is very true that every child faces his and her own seasons. Not all resistance is a direct correlation to the parents' approach. But I can testify it does, over the long haul, make a difference. And the beauty of tender hearts is a joy unlike any other.

These patterns we put into place as parents in cultivating a responsive heart in our children is never more important than in the teenage years. What are the effects if children consistently see mom and dad scream and holler, and pitch a fit over unfinished jobs, toys left on the floor, bickering, or sassy comebacks? Do some of those smaller issues need to be addressed? Probably. But if we set ourselves in motion to rant and rave over every single little issue of childhood, we're setting ourselves up to lose when it comes to the older years. If your children tune you out for your angry outbursts over spilled milk (or even deliberate disobedience) in the young years, you surely can't expect them to listen when you talk about issues of ethics, morality, spiritual growth, sexual purity, and ultimately, the Lordship of Christ. Dr. Francis Schaeffer, in his book *The Great Evangelical Disaster*, emphasized this point of us needing to confront sin in the right way: "God's truth and the work of Christ's church both insist that truth demands loving confrontation, but confrontation."[1]

Angry confrontation is (ouch!) really all about us. Loving confrontation is when we get past ourselves (and our hurt or embarrassment). It's when we partner with the Word of the Lord to bring healing and restoration to wayward young people. We may not be able to change their hearts, much as we'd like to. But the patience, kindness, love, and humility we exhibit, during the painful and needed moments of confrontation, opens the door for the Holy Spirit to come in and do a work.

### In-Season Parenting

Preach the word; be prepared in season and out of season (2 Tim. 4:2).

Do you remember how hard it was to be a parent to a screaming little baby in the middle of the night? We all thought it would be better when they grew up a bit. But then we found some of those same little ones wet their beds at the most inconvenient times, or need a glass of water in the middle of the night, or have a bad dream. Children don't care a thing for the clock. When they need Mom or Dad, it is right now!

With the busy schedules of today's fast-paced world, it seems harder than ever to parent when we feel pressed on all sides by deadlines, agendas, and to-do lists. And boy, oh, boy, if those children should disobey when we are over-the-top busy! It is all too

1. Dr. Francis Schaeffer, *The Great Evangelical Disaster* (in *The Complete Works of Francis Schaeffer, Vol. 4: A Christian View of the Church*) (Westchester, IL: Crossway Books, 1982), p. 402.

easy at such times to let the ugliness of stressed-out parenting come forth in the form of anger.

Yet, here the Scriptures call for us to do all the things parenting is about: preach the Word, correct, rebuke, and encourage — and to do it in season and out of season. I'll tell you what, waking up unexpectedly at 4:00 a.m. with a heart to encourage doesn't come naturally to me. Yet I appreciate the Scripture's counsel and instruction. It causes me to realize that this "in-season" and "out-of-season" parenting needs to be a choice that I make . . . ahead of time . . . when I'm not in the thick of it.

### Lest You, Too, Be Tempted

Galatians 6:1 warns us: "Brothers, if anyone is caught in any transgression, you who are spiritual should restore him in a spirit of gentleness. Keep watch on yourself, lest you too be tempted."

Addressing a child who is destructive, mean-spirited, or even angry himself tends to stir up anger in the parent. We need to watch our own hearts when we are correcting our children.

### Sit Down — What's the Rush?

For some reason, it seems like the "crime scene" with our children happens in inconvenient and uncomfortable places. It's the hallway, or out with the mosquitos in the yard, or in the middle of a messy child's room. Just having to stop the motion of the day and stand to address the situation (and at times having to stare at the crime scene for a length of time) irritates me. Over the years I've come to realize this is an anger trigger for me. So, whenever possible, I invite my youngster to come sit down with me so we can talk. This simple act helps me to focus on my child and his needs, without feeling rushed to correct that child as quickly as possible.

### Limit Your Words

Some of us could put many a university professor to shame, we're *that* good at delivering magnificent, well-versed lectures. Yet, for some reason, our children rarely appreciate our epic speeches, and even turn a deaf ear to them. Angry sermonettes don't truly help parents reach the hearts of their children. In fact, most of the time, parental lectures only benefit the parent as he or she can let off some steam (similar to the end result yelling can have for a parent in which the parent finds release, but the child isn't helped.)

Just as a yelling parent isn't likely to win a listening ear, the lengthy, wordy parent is setting up a scenario for his or her child to shut down. It is important that parents heed the wisdom presented in Proverbs 17:27: "Whoever restrains his words has knowledge, and he who has a cool spirit is a man of understanding."

When we are "hot and bothered" with our young people, the words can come out fast and furious. We get on a roll with our words, and we just don't want to stop! This is where wisdom needs to come into play. The eloquent speech delivered, so we can get it off our chest, isn't going to help our children. You might be 100 percent correct in all you say, and yet still miss delivering the message. Each child is different, and each stage of that child's life will vary. Cool-tempered parents need to recognize when they have lost the child's attention, and curtail their words accordingly. Most of the time, at the point of correction, it is not needful to go into a lengthy discourse about the evils of such behavior. Most likely they already know, based on past experiences, and are disobedient not based on lack of knowledge, but lack of heart-felt obedience.

That said, save your creative lecturing talent for something a little easier to swallow.

### Teach with a Cookie in Hand

Praise God if your child will attentively listen when corrected. For the rest of us, let me encourage you that willingly receiving rebuke is a hard, hard lesson — one that many adults struggle to master! In an effort to help my children toward more responsive hearts,

I've found using "happy" teaching moments can go a long way toward eliminating resistance when correction needs to happen.

So when the sun is shining, and all is right with the world, grab some chocolate chip cookies and preemptively teach your child about the dangers of foolish choices and the rewards of right living. Teach them, when all is cozy and comfortable, what the Bible says about lying and honesty. Share pizza with your teenager and talk sincerely about how you started your walk with the Lord.

Taking the time to teach, talk, and train in a pro-active way means we need to keep our eyes alert for opportune moments. That's really hard to do in the midst of a busy life! But if we don't do it now, during perhaps the busiest season of our lives, when will we?

Second Timothy 4:2 gives further clues just how to go about this: "Preach the word . . . correct, rebuke and encourage — with great patience and careful instruction." Did you notice the words "with great patience" and "careful instruction"? This is the Bible teaching us how to parent!

### Cast a Vision

As we talk with our children, and walk them through seeing where disobedient choices brought them, it is also important to help them see what they could have done right. Oftentimes, the strong emotions of childhood hold such strength that little boys and girls feel compelled to disobey. Many times, the concept of self-control is so foreign, that it will only be through repetitive practice that they "get it." Therefore, practice with your children what good behavior looks like. Talk about how he can tell himself no when the sandbox calls and you've told him to put his bike away. Or how playing with dollies just a few more minutes after you've called for toy pick up, is still delaying obedience. Walking them through, in a fun and fast way, how to heed your words right away, will go a long way toward helping little ones catch on to what you are seeking to instill in them.

Older ones need a different method. As our home is rapidly filling with several teenagers, and up-and-coming young people, we are really thinking about how to help our young people see their place in this world working for Christ. They need a vision that will inspire them in deep and powerful ways to live a meaningful life for Christ. They need to see obedience to the gospel that reaches far beyond the walls of your home. Anytime you yourself can cast this kind of inspiring vision for your young people, it will strengthen them to see godly living is for them, for their lives, for their future. Utilize biographies of Christian leaders, missionary stories, seminars, and videos on evangelism and service. Expand their horizons.

### Draw Close

Anger tends to stand on the opposite side of the room from the offending child. Anger, reared in pride, naturally wants to "get away" from "that child" who has embarrassed, angered, or hurt you. And so, many times, angry parents stand across the room, sending their child a message of disdain. Would you be willing to receive correction from a brother or sister in Christ if he or she came into your home, angrily stared you down, and delivered a harsh correction? I didn't think so.

> *Brook:* One way I have sought physically to show my children that, while the situation needs addressed, I want to see them gain victory, is simply by putting my arm around them. My actions are as much to remind them as to remind myself. Not every child will receive a loving touch, so don't push it if this idea isn't for you.

Similarly, correcting conversations with our children need to be laced with words that create in our children a desire for genuine repentance, right living, and victory over the sin that has beset them. Let your child know that you are *for* him.

This concept of opening the door relationally, even during a difficult conversation, reflects God's heart. All those He disciplines He is treating as sons and daughters. A good question to ask ourselves when we must have correcting conversations with our children is simply, "Am I treating this child as my son or daughter? Or am I treating them with disdain and giving the impression that I don't like them?" God's discipline is always for us — for our good. Hebrews 12:11 says, "For the moment all discipline seems painful rather than pleasant, but later it yields the peaceful fruit of righteousness to those who have been trained by it." Our goal is that the correction we give will point our children toward the peaceful fruit of righteousness as we train them.

Patience, in the way we treat our children, is a powerful force that mirrors God's attitude in Romans 5:8: "But God shows his love for us in that while we were still sinners, Christ died for us" (see also Romans 5:6).

### Use Scripture!

We cut ourselves short when we don't avail ourselves of the mighty Word of God. Second Timothy 3:16 reminds us, directly in this case as parents, just what to use the Word for: "All Scripture is breathed out by God and profitable for teaching, for reproof, for correction, and for training in righteousness." Also, "For the word of God is living and active, sharper than any two-edged sword, piercing to the division of soul and of spirit, of joints and of marrow, and discerning the thoughts and intentions of the heart" (Heb. 4:12).

> **Brook:** I love this passage. So many times as a mother I feel weak, and unable to initiate lasting change in the hearts of my children. Some days I'm not even sure I am coherent. There are days my words seem to come out hollow. Yet God's Word is amazing! It is not lifeless or on bedrest. It is not weak or unintelligible. This Holy Word from a Holy God is alive and powerful, reaching

where parents' words give out, and reaching into the innermost man.

The Scripture goes where we as parents can't seem to reach: "So shall my word be that goes out from my mouth; it shall not return to me empty, but it shall accomplish that which I purpose, and shall succeed in the thing for which I sent it" (Isa. 55:11).

I'm not much for slapping a Bible verse on every childish motion, good or bad, but when addressing core issues of the heart, there is nothing like Scripture to communicate the deep truths of God. Don't neglect to bring the Scriptures to light in your conversations with your children.

### Remember to Pray with and for Your Child

Not every conversation you encounter with your children needs to end in prayer, and not every child will be ready to pray immediately. However, in the busyness of life and the never-ending call to "get back at it," don't neglect the power of praying with your child. As I recently needed to call a young person's heart away from bad habits, I was impressed again with the need for the Holy Spirit to come do the work in my child's heart that I can't seem to pull off. These precious words came back to me from a song I had learned as a child: "Then he said to me, 'This is the word of the LORD to Zerubbabel: Not by might, nor by power, but by my Spirit, says the LORD of hosts'" (Zech. 4:6).

Angry and stressed-out parenting is seeking to build our children using our own might and our own power. We feel like we're "pulling teeth" as we try to drag our youngsters along to conform to "correct" outward behavior. Our might, our angst and rage, our yelling and lecturing, won't capture the hearts of our children. It is through God alone, by the power and might of His Holy Spirit, that our children's hearts will be won over to the Kingdom of God. Ours is a clear path of obedience to partner with Him as He does this work.

### Questions to Consider

Why is it important to replace anger, and not just merely eradicate it?

What is your main goal when you need to correct your child? Are you meeting that goal?

All parents, at some point in their parenting career, are tempted to become angry when correcting their children. What does the Bible say to do in that scenario?

# 10
# The Power of Affirmation

We met a man who visited our church one Sunday. He was a Christian brother who recounted his childhood years with his father. His father was a professional athlete and trained his son to follow in his footsteps. During his growing-up years, this young man did everything he could to measure up to his father's expectations. His father was his role model, and he thought his dad walked on water. However, no matter how hard he worked to please his father, and follow his instructions, he found that he could never measure up.

Nothing he ever did was good enough to meet his father's standards. He never received any affirmation from his dad. He was constantly told that he was not good enough, didn't do something right, or didn't try hard enough. When this young man finally entered his twenties and stepped out from under his father's tutelage, he decided to compete in the sporting field in which his father was a renowned expert.

Much to his surprise, he ended up winning a national competition and being declared the best athlete in his class. Even with this accomplishment, his father still would not admit that he had done anything noteworthy.

### Parenting with a Critical Spirit

If this man's father thought cognitively at all about his approach to raising his son, I suspect he felt he was doing the right thing by his son. He may have felt that he was keeping his son from being soft and complacent. He likely believed that his son would work and try harder if he constantly received an admonition that he could do better. To some extent, this may have been true. Relentlessly pushing his son was doubtless a factor in helping to shape a champion. However, was it worth losing relationship?

The question is, is this the best means for motivating someone? There are two ways to motivate people. One is with positive encouragement and the other with negativity. In terms of leadership styles, it seems that most people excel in one or the other.

I heard another man who had just turned 60 telling a similar tale about his father. He said that the critical spirit in which his father approached him shaped his view of God. When he thinks of God, he thinks of his father. His dad was always one inch away from backhanding him if he got out of line. To this day, he has a hard time believing that God actually *likes* him. He said, "I know God loves me and died for me, but I just can't believe that God actually lights up and smiles when He sees me, because I'm such a mess-up."

### Intrinsic vs. Extrinsic Motivation

There are two basic ways that people can be motivated:

### Intrinsic Motivation — (from within)

The ideal, especially for us as parents, is for our children to want to do the right things *and* for the right reasons. We want them to make positive changes, strive to achieve noble goals, and care for others, simply because they realize it is the right thing to do, and they want to do what is right.

This is sometimes called, "Individual Self-Government." This is our goal. We someday want to see our children embrace all of the things we have tried to teach them and live it out. However, until that day comes, for many parents, they are living in the world of Extrinsic Motivation.

### Extrinsic Motivation — (from without)

When individuals are not self-motivated, they must be prodded from without by an external force. Parents who have children who are not self-starters, and do not take initiative, must seek to inspire them from without. Unfortunately, this often looks an awful lot like policing your children! You have to follow them around, inspecting and making sure they have done everything they were told to do. I don't know about you, but I would eventually enjoy reaching the point in life where I don't have to hunt down my son and say, "Son, it is Tuesday night . . . again. It is now time for you to round up all of the garbage in the house, put it in the trash can, and put it out by the curbside." I would love to see him do it simply because it needs to be done and he cares about it.

If you can relate to this Extrinsic Motivation approach, it will be important for you to remember that there are two approaches you can take to motivating people externally: positive and negative extrinsic motivation.

## Negative Leadership Style

Negative motivation (and correction) is a very powerful force. Cult leaders and dictators use it to keep their followers in line. It isn't always inappropriate or ineffectual. It is something that nearly every parent uses at some point. Even God uses negative motivation in the way He relates to humankind. It has a mighty impact on the human psyche.

The question is, what kind of fruit does this type of parenting approach bear when it is unaccompanied by positive encouragement and affirmation?

Someone with a perennially negative attitude is acidic and repulsive to most people. People tend to try to get away from someone with such an outlook on life. Henry and Richard Blackaby share these powerful insights:

> Cynical leaders cultivate clones of themselves. When leaders have no faith in their people, they prevent them from reaching their potential. . . . Leaders must not allow themselves to be consumed by a scornful spirit, for it will spill over onto everyone around them. True leaders focus on what is right and on what gives hope, not on what is wrong. Unfortunately, criticism or failure, can make a leader skeptical about future success. . . . When leaders sense they are developing a pessimistic attitude, they must correct it immediately before it poisons their

effectiveness and possibly even their health. Without question, a critical spirit in spiritual leaders reveals a heart distant from God. Only a conscious decision to return to God will save the leader from declining into contempt. It is crucial that leaders guard their attitudes. Christian leaders serve the King of kings and therefore have every reason in the world to be positive and optimistic about the future.[1]

While not generally a fan of Bible paraphrases, this rendering of Matthew 7:1–2 (MSG) says what we are trying to communicate here: "Don't pick on people, jump on their failures, criticize their faults — unless, of course, you want the same treatment. That critical spirit has a way of boomeranging."

Charles Schwab, the successful businessman, said, "I have yet to find the man, however exalted his station, who did not do better work and put forth greater effort under a spirit of approval than under a spirit of criticism."[2]

**Positive Leadership Style**

Leadership expert John Maxwell says, "Appreciate people for who they are. This truth is dramatically played out in the lives of children. They have a way of mirroring what they hear about themselves. Recently I watched a talk show which was devoted to the subject of teenage suicide. More and more teenagers are attempting suicide as an escape from the demands of life. They feel they can never measure up to the standards of performance expected by parents and others. They feel appreciated only when they've done well, not because they're unique and priceless individuals. As a result, many kids see life as a no-win situation."[3]

---

1. Henry and Richard Blackaby, *Spiritual Leadership: Moving People on to God's Agenda* (Nashville, TN: B & H Publishing, 2011), Kindle version, p. 324–325.
2. https://www.goodreads.com/author/quotes/207029.Charles_Schwab.
3. John C. Maxwell, *Be a People Person: Effective Leadership Through Effective Relationships* (Colorado Springs, CO: David C. Cook, 2007), p. 163–164.

God, as our Heavenly Father, sets the perfect example for us when He says: "This is my beloved Son, in whom I am well pleased" (Matt. 3:17).

> *The most important time to affirm people, and be a cheerleader, is when they are moving out and stretching. Too many people affirm too late. . . . (R)emember that even a tombstone will say good things about a fellow after he's dead. Don't be a tombstone encourager. Affirm early. Affirm often. Don't wait for the race to be won, but encourage each step forward. Affirm immediately. The effect of an encouraging word loses its strength as time lapses. . . . Affirm personally, and don't be afraid to affirm in front of others. Nothing is more encouraging than to receive honest praise in front of your peers.*[4]

### Heart Check

Do your children know that you are well pleased with them? Are you someone who has a pleasant disposition and a ready smile? Are you enjoyable to be around? If so, your home will be haven of peace. In contrast, consider the woman in Proverbs 25:24: "It is better to live in a corner of the roof than in a house shared with a contentious woman" (NASB).

When your child needs to be corrected, there should be no severity, anger, or violence involved; no contempt or disgust. You should address the action or behavior without attacking the person.

> Do not let any unwholesome talk come out of your mouths, but only what is helpful for building others up according to their needs, that it may benefit those who listen. ... Get rid of all bitterness, rage and anger, brawling and slander, along with every form of malice (Eph. 4:29–31).

---

4. John Maxwell, *Be All You Can Be* (Colorado Springs, CO: David C. Cook, 2007), p. 44–45, emphasis added.

Do you tend to focus on the failure of your children? Do you look at your own life/faults through a telescope, but at your child's with a microscope? Do you have low expectations of your children? Do you expect your children to fail? Does fault finding come easier to you than praise? Do you speak down to your children in a condescending manner? Do you have a demanding spirit? Do you have a need to point out every time your children does something imperfectly? Do you find yourself more frequently looking for reasons to correct your children than to catch them in the act of doing something commendable?

### From Where Does a Critical Attitude Come?

- **Overload** — In many cases, a negative attitude comes out of a sense of being overwhelmed. Most of us are overcommitted and have too many activities and responsibilities we are trying to juggle. We need to find ways to simplify, downscale, and reduce. We need to create margin, white space, silence, and solitude in our lives in order to create balance.

- **Repeating the Cycle** — Many times, a negative person is just repeating the cycle of their own childhood. We tend to parent in the way we were parented. Even if we dislike the way our parents treated us, we often perpetuate the same habits and attitudes to the next generation.

- **Aging** — "Older (people) seem particularly susceptible to cynicism. Their youthful enthusiasm has worn off, and what they consider 'realism born of experience' may in essence be nothing more than a cynical attitude that has festered over time."[5]

- **Feeling Alone** — People who feel alone often respond in frustration with others. Many mothers feel

---

5. Blackaby, *Spiritual Leadership: Moving People on to God's Agenda*, Kindle version, p. 324–325

this sense of being alone, even in a house full of people. Often, they feel that they are the only ones with a vision, a burden, or a desire to see things improved or accomplished. A mother sometimes feels as though she is trying to pull a heavy wooden cart uphill, all by herself, and her children aren't willing to help. And her husband is sitting in the cart giving directions on how she could do it all better! This results in negative feelings toward those around them (or those they believe should be helping or cooperating).

- **Impatience** — Often, parents do not properly understand the capability of their child. They expect more than what their child is able to deliver given their age and/or physical/mental/emotional abilities. Sometimes we want instant progress or immediate results. Parenting is not a sprint, it is a marathon. We win in the long run, incrementally, through a thousand little victories. Impatience is rooted in wanting life to happen on your time schedule (which it seldom does). Remember that patience is something that is only gained by abiding in Christ and allowing the fruit of His Spirit to flow through us.

- **Spiritual Depletion** — The fruit of the Spirit (see Galatians 5) is the opposite of a harsh, critical spirit. If you are not daily abiding in the life of Jesus, and allowing His divine power to flow through your life, you will be frustrated and will take that frustration out on others. Joy, hope, kindness, mercy, and love *only* flow out of the power of the Spirit of the living God.

The secret to bearing spiritual fruit is abiding in Jesus. That means you need to find time to spend alone with Jesus every single day. You cannot continue to give to others and serve them if you are not taking time to refuel yourself. We all have so many demands on our time, but this cannot be neglected.

Susanna Wesley gave birth to 19 children, two of whom were famous evangelist John Wesley, and renowned hymn writer Charles Wesley (founders of the Methodist movement). Living in a small house with many children, it was often difficult for Susanna to find a quick place to spend time alone with the Lord. So she would occasionally, in a stressful moment, take her apron and throw it over her head so she could have five minutes alone to talk to Jesus. Her children understood that when mom was having "apron time," she was not to be interrupted!

We can't tell you what this refueling time will look like for you, but we strongly encourage you to seek out ways to maintain daily spiritual disciplines. Your spiritual growth hinges on it.

### A Future and a Hope

Speaking gently and kindly to our children is not an area in which most of us excel. Sometimes we realize that we are not doing what is right, but we find ourselves resorting to a default mode of fault finding and being critical rather than constructive.

Over time, the net result of this approach of negativity is that your children will disrespect you, tune out, quit trying, and seek to avoid contact and communication with you. People tend to seek out those who will affirm and inspire them, not those who will constantly point out their flaws and drag them down.

It has been said that parents should give ten positive statements of affirmation for any one statement of correction. That is a tall order, but it shows the heart of balance in this regard.

The goal is *not* to ignore sin and laziness in our children. The goal is *not* to build a false sense of self-esteem that is disconnected from reality. The goal is *not* to avoid any kind of confrontation at all costs. The goal is *not* to be negligent in pointing out and upholding a standard.

However, the more important goal is that we are godly ourselves, *not* that we make everyone else godly. If we are truly living as Christ wants us to, in our attitudes and actions, *that* will be successfully transferred to our children, regardless of what we say. More is caught than taught in parenting. Whatever we do in our approach to parenting must be rooted in a deep and abiding sacrificial love for our children, and never out of a sense of our own comfort or security.

There is no need to live in defeat in this area. "His divine power has given us everything we need for a godly life through our knowledge of him who called us by his own glory and goodness" (2 Pet. 1:3; NIV). By God's grace, we can learn to be encouragers (those who inspire courage) rather than those who discourage (take away courage and inspire defeat).

### Questions to Consider

What would you say your leadership style tends to reflect the most: positive or negative motivation?

What are ways you have or would like to inspire intrinsic motivation in your children?

Have you felt that spiritual depletion might be a component in your relationship with your children? Why or why not? If so, what is one simple thing you can do today to feed yourself spiritually?

# 11

# Creating Peace
# in the Home

Anger squelches joy and gives it no chance to grow. If anger has infiltrated your home, the tension might be so thick that joy seems like something out of reach. This is just the kind of situation God wants to work in, because He is the God of the impossible. He isn't looking around for happy, well-adjusted homes to heal — He is looking for the sick, the lost, the despairing (see Luke 5:31).

While the miracle He wants to see happen in our families may be a long time in coming, it only takes one person to get the ball rolling. His peace that passes all understanding might be found at first in the simplicity of these words: "If possible, so far as it depends on you, live peaceably with all" (Rom. 12:18). Hebrews 12:14 says this: "Strive for peace with everyone, and for the holiness without which no one will see the Lord."

### Gratefulness for Our Children

A peaceful home doesn't happen overnight. Anytime you have two humans together there is potential for conflict. But then add several small humans, and well, let's just say achieving a peaceful home becomes a challenge! Home is where our families know us as we really are. They see everything. And we see our children's weaknesses at every stage. In the daily grind, as we all rub each other the wrong way at times, it can be easy to become rather ho-hum about the precious value of our children.

Thankfulness for our children plays a big part in our turning from angry parenting. When we truly recognize that these children are not "our" children, but rather God's children, a sense of respect and carefulness is bound to enter into our parenting. God's vested interest in our children is greater than even the strongest bond between parent and child. We play a part in giving our children life, yet God is the One who creates each life! He cares intensely how we treat these children of *His*. As basic as it sounds, simple gratefulness to God for the children with whom He has entrusted us can be an asset in helping us turn from anger in our relationships to a greater awareness of God's hand on these children we call our own. Gratefulness turns our attention from *us*, and our rights or irritations, to the call of God on our lives to raise our children.

### The Greatest of These Is Love

The very end of 1 Corinthians chapter 13 tells us, "So now faith, hope, and love abide, these three; but the greatest of these is love." Do we need faith to overcome anger? We sure do! Do we need hope? Yes. But the greatest need of all is love. We've got to have love to overcome anger. Love is met in every one of the fruits of the Spirit. It is a powerful antidote to anger. Just look over this list:

- Love
- Joy
- Peace
- Patience
- Kindness
- Goodness
- Faithfulness
- Gentleness
- Self-control

These are ways of God, and wow, if we can get them into our way of living, they will have a far-reaching impact for good on our children. Throughout the Scriptures we're told to love one another (the Books of John and 1 John are particularly full of this command!).

### God Has His Part and We Have Our Part

We're told to "put away" anger (Col. 3:8) and to "put on" our new self (Col. 3:10). The Scriptures are clear that we have a choice in all of this. Yes, this is an amazing work of God in us. Praise Him for that!

> And I am sure of this, that he who began a good
> work in you will bring it to completion at the day of
> Jesus Christ (Phil. 1:6).

> For it is God who works in you, both to will and to
> work for his good pleasure (Phil. 2:13).

But we also play a tremendous part in whether we embrace the
work He is doing in us or not. Sometimes we just have to walk out
the thing we know to be true until it becomes a habitual part of us.
Loving our children in their unlovable moments may not come
easily at first, but over time, doing the right thing can become our
default position.

In Colossians 3:5, we are told to "put to death" what is of our
fleshly nature.

> And those who belong to Christ Jesus have crucified
> the flesh with its passions and desires (Gal. 5:24).

We are not powerless over the anger we allow to rule us, strong as
it is. Learning how to die to old nature, and to come alive in the
newness of the Spirit, is our final aim.

### Never Give Up!

This fight (war!) that we have against anger in parenting can be a
very difficult one. While many times parents cringe, feeling they
are losing against the battle of anger, there are other parents who
give up in an entirely different way.

Growing up, my family interacted with a family with several
children. Their oldest daughter, as most eldest children are prone
to be, was a bit stubborn, and that's putting it mildly. Having
sought, rather unsuccessfully, to corral her stubborn temper
by matching it with their own anger, the mom and dad finally
decided to ditch the whole concept of parental guidance. Because
they "loved their daughter so much" and earnestly wanted to
keep her heart by not becoming angry at her, they simply stopped

crossing their daughter. After that, the parents were as calm as could be in the face of her rebellion. They never said no. They didn't seek to guide her.

On the surface, their attempts seem valiant, because at least they weren't losing their cool, yet Proverbs says such parents actually hate their own children. "But he who loves him is diligent to discipline him" (Prov. 13:24). True to form, this gal lived out Proverbs 29:15, ". . . a child left to himself brings shame to his mother," and brought much heartache to her family through drug addictions, multiple failed marriages, and major financial instability.

Simply choosing not to interact in meaningful ways with our children, or provide boundaries, doesn't really provide a cure for anger. It might stifle it temporarily, but it always translates as disinterest to the children affected by it.

Sometimes we've been wrongly led to believe that to avoid anger we must sacrifice any sort of standard and become a human doormat for our children. The whole thrust of this book has been to encourage parents that there are nurturing, loving, kind ways of walking our children toward obedience apart from anger. Anger is focused primarily on the outward behavior, but nurturing parenting is all about getting at the heart. The two can exist together: "Steadfast love and faithfulness meet; righteousness and peace kiss each other" (Ps. 85:10).

### Kicking Anger Out of Your Parenting Team

All too often, when one parent is angry, the spouse despises him or her for that weakness. They look on with disgust when a spouse is angry. Do you remember though how closely related pride is to anger? It is almost as if the two can't bear to be apart. Even when you are not the angry party, just seeing it can invoke all kinds of feelings of pride. ("I'm glad *I'm* not like that!" or "Wow, what a fool he or she is making of herself! *I* wouldn't do that!") Pride seeks distance from someone "beneath" us. Humility seeks to come close and spread the good news of hope and patience.

Marriage is supposed to be teamwork, and at no other time is it as needed as in the parenting journey. God's normal system is that both parents work together in the process of spiritual growth and maturity. Sure, God's grace can cover situations that involve an unregenerate spouse, or a spouse who is not, for whatever reason, engaged relationally, but His original plan was for us to work in tandem with . . . (shock!) an imperfect person.

This is where humility has to kick in. You married an imperfect person, and you are an imperfect person. Sometimes your husband or wife will need to say something to you that you don't want to hear (but you know is the truth). At other times, the tables may be turned. Remember how you'd like to be treated when it is your turn to speak, and give that kind of gentle reminder.

Way too many husbands and wives act autonomously in the parenting marathon. Husbands put down their wives in front of the children, and wives undermine their husband's fatherhood by tearing him down as well. Even humor is often used as mask for anger. We've seen people make cutting statements about their spouse in public, but doing it under the guise of humor. If they are ever challenged on it they can attempt to back down and say, "I was only joking!" The problem is, it isn't funny. Passive aggressive anger disguised as humor, or cloaked in sarcasm, is still a way to wound your spouse, and it destroys intimacy.

Anger and pride in your parenting team will cause you to lose every time. Humility is the way to victory.

Another area that parents allow anger to get in the way of their teamwork is by playing off of one another's angry emotions. Say Dad becomes angry about some job a child has left undone, which has already been irritating Mom for several hours. Now Mom, fueled by Dad's anger, is ready to let that child have an earful of her pent-up frustrations! Soon enough, the whole house is on edge! Simply recognizing this as a possible trigger can help you "get an edge" and come up with solution (a teamwork solution between husband and wife who both want to overcome anger). Don't forget the power of employing Proverbs 15:1. Take some time to look that passage up and consider it.

Could I recommend that the two of you read this book, and other books on anger, together? Even if one of you doesn't struggle in this area, reading aloud can create good fuel for conversations. Maybe where words fail you, you can point to something you are reading together and say, "This is where I want to go. Please help me, gently!"

> Two are better than one, because they have a good reward for their toil. For if they fall, one will lift up his fellow. But woe to him who is alone when he falls and has not another to lift him up! Again, if two lie together, they keep warm, but how can one keep warm alone? And though a man might prevail against one who is alone, two will withstand him — a threefold cord is not quickly broken (Eccles. 4:9–12).

### A Partnership

We are in a covenant relationship with the raising of our children. We are in covenant with God, and in covenant with each other, as a married couple. Unity in our marriage goes a long way toward our being effective in reaching our children's hearts. A united front is so much more powerful than two people working against each other.

If you find that you and your spouse are not on the same page, and are actually working against each other, take whatever steps are necessary to seek counseling through your local church elders and/or a qualified biblical counselor. Having a strong marriage is one of the best things you could ever do for your children. Don't neglect your marriage in the process of trying to raise your children. Keep first things first. Keep Christ first, your marriage second, and your outreach to your children a unified third.

### Questions to Consider

Do you allow your children to be a source of joy to you? Or are you bent on perfection? Do their personalities irk you?

What are some ways that you and your spouse could have some honest and vulnerable discussions with each other as you seek together to rid your home of angry parenting?

Are there ways in which angry parenting stems from anger in your marriage? What are principles you've learned about eradicating anger from your parenting that you could apply to your marriage?

# 12

# Accountability

> Therefore, since we are surrounded by so great a cloud of witnesses, let us also lay aside every weight, and sin which clings so closely, and let us run with endurance the race that is set before us, looking to Jesus, the founder and perfecter of our faith (Heb. 12:1–2).

If this topic of anger and stressed-out parenting brings conviction to you, praise God! He is working in you and treating you as His child! This short passage in Hebrews brings such hope and compassion for a heart such as yours:

> . . . but he [God] disciplines us for *our good*, that we may share *his holiness*. For the moment all discipline seems painful rather than pleasant, but later it yields the *peaceful fruit* of righteousness to those who have been *trained by it* (Heb.12:10–11, emphasis added).

How great that the discipline He gives us is so that we may share in His holiness. He wants us to become like Himself — full of love and patience. Hebrews declares that this discipline later yields the *peaceful* fruit (note: not angry or stressed out) of righteousness. This wonderful fruit is for those who have been trained by it. Throughout these pages, we've discussed several ways we can incorporate habits that defy anger. Some of these ideas may work for you, but each of us, and each of our families, are unique. These pages are meant to be a prompt toward allowing God to work in you His patience and love, to weed out the anger, and to train you in new habits of nurture.

### Untended Anger Will Take You Down

The world around us sends confusing messages about anger, some of which seek to tame the consequences of this sin too much. On one hand, everyone denounces angry parenting as harmful to a child, yet on the other hand, they cling to a fuzzy standard by calling it "normal." Of course, we all like to be told that parental anger is just a "phase" that is typical for our age group, and that we'll eventually outgrow it. But is it true? Will we really just "outgrow" anger?

The fact is, a lifestyle of anger is no joke. It *will* take you down if you let it. It *will* take your family down if something is not done about it. Anger doesn't like to be kept in a nice tidy box in the broom closet — it grows and oozes out and seeks to destroy us and our families. Proverbs 6:27 puts it this way: "Can a man carry fire next to his chest and his clothes not be burned?"

We can't maintain a condoning attitude toward anger and not expect it to negatively affect our families.

### Broken Walls

Have you ever seen old photos from the excavated ruins of ancient Israel? Or for that matter, of ancient Rome with her cities flung around the Mediterranean, Europe, and Asia Minor? These cities of old were built with huge, towering walls surrounding the entire perimeter of the city. Guards were stationed atop the walls at key points, and entrances to the city were closely watched at the gates. These walls brought a sense of comfort to the citizens. When they left their homes to tend their household garden, or allow their little ones some exercise, or draw some water from the nearest well, or work or shop in the market place, there was no need to fearfully watch to see if any enemies approached. The walls were strong, the guards alert, the gates secure. These city walls provided protection.

But listen to what Proverbs 25:28 says: "A person without self-control is like a city with broken-down walls" (NLT). A city without a wall was laid open for attack from any traveling army. The enemy could swarm upon its people from any direction. There was no guard to stand watch and give out an alarm should the enemy approach from a distance.

Lack of self-control leaves the field wide open for the enemy of our souls to gain access to our families. As parents, we work so hard to provide safety for our children's physical bodies; yet if self-control is missing, it is as if we are opening the door for danger to come near our children.

### Seek Accountability

How do you know if your anger habits are severe enough that you need to seek outside assistance and accountability? Here are a few symptoms that things have progressed beyond the point where you are able to manage them yourself:

1. If you yell every day
2. If your child does not connect (reconnect) with you emotionally and relationally (they have withdrawn from you in some way)
3. If you feel out of control when angry
4. If you are abusive to your children
5. If anger isn't an infrequent, short-lived occurrence, but an ongoing lifestyle

The first line of defense against anger should, ideally, be your own spouse. This is the truest, and safest place to live out Proverbs 27:17 ("Iron sharpens iron, and one man sharpens another"). However, sometimes your spouse is just as caught up in anger as you are (or worse). Or some parents have the unenviable job of trying to fill the difficult single-parent role. Also, sometimes a spouse spends much time away from home because of military or business travel.

If this kind of accountability is not available to you, look for a trusted, godly friend who will pray with you, challenge you, and encourage you, preferably someone in an older season of life than you. Now, let me add a word of caution: It is really too easy to look for someone who will comfort us in our distress and kindly tell us, "Oh, that's all right, everything will turn out just fine." We believe the ideal scenarios would be your church elders working with you as a married couple, or an older woman teaching the younger woman as described in Titus 2:3–5. The local church is, ideally, the place where we should look for help, encouragement, and accountability. However, we realize that, for various reasons, sometimes that wise and trusted counsel and wisdom is not always available through your local church, so we also recommend seeking a qualified biblical counselor. Consider finding one in your area from BiblicalCounseling.com.

In order to help clarify what exactly you are asking your friend to do, it may be helpful to explain that you have identified anger as a real problem in your life, and you want to be held accountable for the purpose of changing. Hopefully, your accountability partner or counselor will recommend resources, and perhaps provide you with assignments. They will possibly also ask you these questions from time to time:

1. What have you done about the anger you had this week?

2. What will you do about the anger you had this week?

3. What Scriptures apply to the situation that made you angry? How would you handle it if you had to do it over again?

4. Have you made restitution and reconnected with your child?

### Can't I Be Accountable to My Children?

We have some concerns about employing one's children as accountability partners. We've heard parents say they have asked their children to let them know if he or she is acting angry so that the parent can be reminded to stop. Personally, we think being Mommy or Daddy's accountability partner is too much responsibility to put on young shoulders. Older and wiser shoes than a child have had difficulty filling the role of a mentor. If you simply need a little reminder to keep yourself in check, put it on yourself to be the one to tell yourself "no" or "stop." Ask the Holy Spirit to remind you. If you need someone to make you give an account for your attitude and actions, then find someone suited for the task. Finally, it doesn't make sense to us that if a parent is addressing a child and losing his or her cool, that a simple reminder from said child would really help them step off the angry ladder.

We also have concerns about asking one's children to be accountability partners because it skews with the authority structure of a parent as a leader in their child's life. When a child is put in the place, now and then, to be Mom or Dad's authority and tell them when to stop or point out their bad behavior, it can create a sense of superiority. That's too difficult to balance. These children tend to begin rejecting their mom or dad, developing a really low view of them.

Conversely, if your children see you diligently working on your besetting sins and weaknesses, you will rise in their estimation. Similarly, when you can humble yourself and repent for the ways you have sinned against them, healing and trust can begin to happen.

Here's what one mom has to say: "So I spent my morning tidying up the house and spent the majority of my time in the kitchen. . . . After finishing up, I went out front to sit and enjoy watching the kids while they played. Cade was thirsty and went inside to pour himself a cup of tea and his younger siblings followed him inside. A few moments later, Cade comes outside and told me he'd spilled the tea. I jump up and run inside to find almost a half-gallon of sweet tea all over my counters and floor.

"I lost it. I yelled. I gave dirty looks and was just plain . . . annoyed. As I started to clean up I felt the 'tap on my shoulder.' (You know, the one where God says, 'Look.') As I saw three sets of wide eyes and hurt hearts, I put down the towel and just said . . . 'I am so sorry.' The words I shared with my littles are between me and them. But I just realized in that moment, I. Was. Wrong. It's tea for heaven's sake! I was tearing down my littles over tea. Needless to say, I made the offense right with them. My big seven-year-old son wanted to help by pouring not only himself a drink but also for his brother and sister. What an amazing little man he is! What a *huge* mom fail for me. I'm not telling you this or even apologizing to make you think what a great mom I am. I'm doing it because I want *them* to feel like they have a great mom. Love those tiny humans you've been entrusted with and just let the little spills go. Your babies are far more important."

### Seek it Like You Mean It!

The deal with accountability is that it is only as good as you want it to be. It's only as effective as your desire to actually change. If you lie to your accountability partner, under-represent your struggle, fail to admit that you have an anger problem, justify your actions, etc., you won't change. Simple as that. It is only once you finally get really desperately tired of being a slave to your anger that you will finally take the steps necessary to break free.

Some people go to weekly addiction meetings with a support group and never get victory, even after years of group-counseling sessions. Why? Because simply "managing" your anger isn't going to cut it. You can't just say, week after week, "Well, I blew it again. I guess I'll just try harder to do better this next week."

At a certain point, you must believe that what you are doing is not healthy and that God is not okay with your behavior. Then you must believe that, through Christ, you can and will find substantive victory in your life over your anger addiction. If you don't believe that, then you will stay stuck. Forever. You will never change until you believe it is possible to be different that you are right now.

We aren't talking about absolute perfection, where you never mess up again for as long as you live. Instead, we are insisting that substantive life change is possible through the power of Christ.

> And without faith it is impossible to please him, for whoever would draw near to God must believe that he exists and that he rewards those who seek him (Heb. 11:6).

If you want God to move on your behalf, you need to trust Him and put your full confidence in Him.

> If any of you lacks wisdom, let him ask God, who gives generously to all without reproach, and it will be given him. But let him ask in faith, with no doubting, for the one who doubts is like a wave of the sea that is driven and tossed by the wind. For that person must not suppose that he will receive anything from the Lord; he is a double-minded man, unstable in all his ways (James 1:5–8).

If you don't expect God to answer your prayers, don't bother to pray them, because He won't.

> You will seek me and find me, when you seek me with all your heart (Jer. 29:13).

Victory will not ultimately come through tips and techniques (as important as these may be in your process), or even through a counselor or an accountability partner. Only God can change a heart, and the heart is the only place where true change can ultimately occur. God can, and will, impart His nature in you and teach you to become like Him in His holiness. That is what sanctification is all about, and it is available to every redeemed believer, through the power of the Holy Spirit living inside of you. Believe it! Expect great things from God! Thank God for every little victory!

### Questions to Consider

Read more in Hebrews 12:1–15.

Can you think of a time God disciplined you?

Who is someone you know (a mature Christian) who walks in the peace of Christ, that you could contact to seek wisdom, advice, and counsel regarding your anger struggle?

What are questions you could add to the list in the chapter to give to a mentor when you need counsel regarding anger?